PENGUIN CLASSICS

"SPAIN, TAKE THIS CHALICE FROM ME"
AND OTHER POEMS

CÉSAR VALLEJO was born the youngest of eleven children in Peru in 1892. He published his first book of poems, *Los heraldos negros*, in 1919, and a second book, *Trilce*, in 1922, which is still considered to be one of the most avant-garde collections of poetry in the Spanish language. He spent the bulk of his life living in Europe, namely Paris, where he contributed to weeklies in France, Lima, Spain, and Italy. After becoming emotionally and intellectually involved in the Spanish Civil War, he had a final burst of poetic energy in the late 1930s, writing two books, *Poemas Humanos* and *España, aparta de mí este cáliz,* both of which were published posthumously. Vallejo died in dire poverty in Paris on April 15, 1938, of an unknown illness, now thought to have been a form of malaria.

MARGARET SAYERS PEDEN has translated over sixty books by such major Latin American authors as Isabel Allende, Sor Juana Inés de la Cruz, Carlos Fuentes, Pablo Neruda, and Octavio Paz, and is Professor Emeritus of Spanish at the University of Missouri.

ILAN STAVANS is the Lewis-Sebring Professor in Latin American and Latino Culture and Five-College 40th Anniversary Professor at Amherst College. His books include *The Hispanic Condition* (1995), *The Riddle of Cantinflas* (1997), *The Essential Ilan Stavans* (2000), *On Borrowed Words* (2001), *Spanglish* (2003), *Dictionary Days* (2005), *The Disappearance* (2006), and *Love and Language* (2007). He is the editor of, among other works, *Growing Up Latino* (1994), *The Oxford Book of Latin American Essays* (1997), and *The Poetry of Pablo Neruda* (2003). He is the recipient of numerous awards and honors, including a Guggenheim Fellowship, the Latino Hall of Fame Award, Chile's Presidential Medal, the Rubén Darío Medal, and the National Jewish Book Award. Stavans writes a newspaper column syndicated throughout the Spanish-speaking world.

CÉSAR VALLEJO

"Spain, Take This Chalice from Me" and Other Poems

Translated by
MARGARET SAYERS PEDEN
Edited with an Introduction by
ILAN STAVANS

PENGUIN BOOKS

PENGUIN BOOKS

Published by the Penguin Group

Penguin Group (USA) Inc., 375 Hudson Street, New York, New York 10014, U.S.A.

Penguin Group (Canada), 90 Eglington Avenue East, Suite 700, Toronto, Ontario, Canada M4P 2Y3 (a division of Pearson Penguin Canada Inc.)

Penguin Books Ltd, 80 Strand, London WC2R 0RL, England

Penguin Ireland, 25 St Stephen's Green, Dublin 2, Ireland (a division of Penguin Books Ltd)

Penguin Group (Australia), 250 Camberwell Road, Camberwell, Victoria 3124, Australia (a division of Pearson Australia Group Pty Ltd)

Penguin Books India Pvt Ltd, 11 Community Centre, Panchsheel Park, New Delhi – 110 017, India

Penguin Group (NZ), 67 Apollo Drive, Rosedale, North Shore 0632, New Zealand (a division of Pearson New Zealand Ltd)

Penguin Books (South Africa) (Pty) Ltd, 24 Sturdee Avenue, Rosebank, Johannesburg 2196, South Africa

Penguin Books Ltd, Registered Offices:
80 Strand, London WC2R 0RL, England

This edition first published in Penguin Books 2008

1   3   5   7   9   10   8   6   4   2

Translation copyright © Margaret Sayers Peden, 2008
Introduction copyright © Ilan Stavans, 2008
All rights reserved

ISBN 978-0-14-310530-5
CIP data available

Printed in the United States of America
Set in Sabon

Qui potest capere capiat.
—El Evangelio

He who is able to receive it, let him receive it.
—Matthew 19:12

Contents

CONTENTS

Introduction

Refuse symmetry as certainty.
—Trilce XXXVI

César Vallejo stands as a towering figure in twentieth-century Spanish-language poetry, an innovator, an engaged artist with a revolutionary feeling not only for syntax and style but for the political events of his time. His visionary spirit is clear from his first collection, *Black Heralds*. At this time he was still in his native Peru. His monumental *Trilce* was released after he was imprisoned for his involvement in a street riot, and his vision remained bright and clear in the last words he penned: the poems collected in *Posthumous Poems,* which include the cycle *Spain, Take This Chalice from Me,* about the Spanish Civil War, which he witnessed firsthand before his death in 1938, at the age of forty-six. In the transition between his earliest efforts and the ones he worked on toward the end, the reader is able to appreciate a reconfiguration of language so ambitious in scope that it isn't a misrepresentation to call Vallejo the most radical word weaver in Hispanic America.

And arguably among the most hermetic, too—or maybe the right term is *esoteric.* Mario Vargas Llosa, also a Peruvian, once argued that Vallejo eludes the efforts of the rational mind to make sense of his poems. It isn't that he is inexplicable, the author of *Aunt Julia and the Script Writer* believes, but that the nucleus of Vallejo's message appears to be irreducible to simple qualities as organized by our intellect. "[His] poetry, for all its references to familiar landscapes and a social and historical milieu, transcends those coordinates of time and space and positions the reader on a more permanent and profound plane: that of the human condition," states Vargas Llosa. "Which is to say, the existential reality of which the lives of men and women are made: the uncertainty about our origin and our future beyond this earth; and also the intensity of our emotions when we are overcome by love, excitement, pity, or nostalgia. But the mystery of his poetry resides not in those existential subjects or states but, rather, in how they take shape in a language that communicates them to the reader directly, more through a sort of osmosis or contagion than through any intelligible discourse."

Vallejo is known as a *vanguardista*. Etymologically, the term *vanguardia* derives from *avant-garde,* an Anglicized French military term, archaic in its original use, which, according to the *Oxford English Dictionary,* described "the foremost part of an army," the section made of skilled soldiers entrusted with reconnaissance missions. But at the time of Surrealism the word, meaning front guard, was used to describe experimental, aesthetically radical artistic trends, even art for art's sake. In this vein Vallejo's radical poetry must be seen in context. Prior to him, at the end of the nineteenth century, an aesthetic movement called *modernismo,* led by Nicaraguan poet and diplomat Rubén Darío and Cuban writer and freedom fighter José Martí, established Latin American letters not as an offshoot of Iberian literature but as an innovative, cosmopolitan pan-Hispanic trend. Roughly circumscribed between 1885 and 1915, the *modernistas* accomplished an astonishing feat: They created a continental camaraderie while, at the same time, their group was taken seriously in Spain. Infatuated as they were with French Symbolism and Parnassianism, Darío and his colleagues (José Santos Chocano from Peru, as well as Julio Herrera y Reissig from Uruguay, Manuel Gutiérrez Nájera from Mexico, Julián del Casal from Cuba, and José Asunción Silva from Colombia, among others) infused *el español* with a sense of uniqueness.

Born barely four years after the publication of Darío's *Azul . . . ,* the most influential of the *modernista* books, Vallejo was suckled by the *modernista* revolution. He harbored a deep admiration for Darío. In his poem "Retable" he describes himself as moving against the current, "escaping from the noise," alone while "no one sees that I'm going to the sacred nave" where "tall shadows gather, / and Darío goes by with his mourning-draped lyre." Later on in the same piece, he describes the Nicaraguan as "Darío of the celestial Americas!" Indeed, his role, as he realized while composing the poems of *Black Heralds* (a title that invokes Darío's *Los heraldos*), is to take the effort further into the realm of introspection. The push further also meant a move away from the decorative nature of Darío's swans and princesses and toward an introspection that would make language less flashy, more elastic. The opening poem in the collection, also called "Black Heralds," has an existential tenor to it. The first poem is justifiably famous; although more mechanical and bombastic than his mature oeuvre, it encapsulates Vallejo's career-long motifs (Catholicism, an obsession with death and silence, etc.) and showcases his debt to Darío, in particular to his poem *"Lo fatal."* It also announces what is to come in the collection:

There are blows in life, so formidable . . . I don't know!
Blows as if from God's hatred; as if when struck
the undertow from everything ever suffered
were forming wells in your soul . . . I don't know!

They are few, but they are . . . they open dark gullies
in the fiercest face and strongest back.
Perhaps they are the colts of barbarous Atillas;
or the black heralds sent to us by Death.

They are profound lapses of the Christs of the soul,
of some exalted faith that Destiny blasphemes.
Those blood-soaked blows are crepitations
from bread burning at the oven door.

And man . . . Poor . . . creature! His eyes turn back, as
when someone claps us on the shoulder;
his crazed eyes turn back, and all that he has lived
forms a well, like a pool of guilt, in his gaze.

There are blows in life, so formidable . . . I don't know!

But *Trilce* is a far more daring contribution. Saúl Yurkievich once said that "there are few books in contemporary literature in Spanish with . . . as much innovation and poetic quality." It is a manifesto on the limits of language and an exploration of consciousness. Published the year before Borges' first book, *Fervor de Buenos Aires,* it was an explosion that arrived, clearly, before its time. Plus, it's important to remember that in the context of English-language Modernism the year 1922 marks the publication of James Joyce's *Ulysses* and T. S. Eliot's *The Waste Land.* Its first edition, released in Peru, was either ignored or misunderstood. It was the second one, made in Spain, with a prologue by José Bergamín, which brought it to the attention of a small cadre of passionate readers and, in due course, dramatically expanded its circle of influence.

César Abraham Vallejo was born on March 16, 1892, in Santiago de Chuco, a small mining town in the northern Andes mountains. (There are some who claim he was born on March 7. And his first tombstone erroneously listed 1893 as his birth year.) The youngest of eleven children, he was raised in a close-knit Catholic family and, according to his early biographer, André Coyné, he dreamed of becoming a priest.

Vallejo's Indian looks and consciousness defined his identity. He was a *cholo,* a term of essential currency in Peru. The *Diccionario de la Lengua Española* of the Real Academia Española de la Lengua defines the word thus: *"Mestizo de sangre europea o indígena,"* a person of mixed European or Amerindian blood. Other lexicons are more elusive, such as *Clave: Diccionario del uso del español actual.* It states: *"En zonas del español meridional, indio o mestizo occidentalizados."* The distinction is categorical as it suggests a word used in the Andean region to describe a Westernized Indian or *mestizo.* Vallejo was a member of the lower class. Ethnically, he was a mixture of European and Quechua ancestry. But although he identified with his Indian roots, he looked to Europe for inspiration. He wasn't expected to pursue a college education. Still, his passion for literature and learning led him to a job as a teacher at the Centro Escolar de Varones and Colegio Nacional de San Juan.

He had a sorrowful, melancholic side to his character noticeable by those around him. Ciro Alegría, the author of *El mundo es ancho y ajeno* (The World Is Wide and Foreign) and one of Vallejo's students at the Colegio Nacional de San Juan, once said that "from his whole being there flowed a deep sadness." Pablo Neruda, who met him in France in the twenties and toward whom Vallejo at first was attracted but then became hostile (in a letter written the year before his death, he described the Chilean as *"ligero, demagógico e interesado,"* light, demagogical, and selfish), called him "the great *cholo,"* and said that Vallejo was "a poet whose poetry had a rough surface, as rugged to the touch as a wild animal's skin, but it was magnificent poetry with extraordinary power." Read attentively, Neruda's comments have a certain air of condescension: He doesn't talk about Vallejo's poetry but about his aboriginal features. In his *Memoirs,* Neruda writes (in Margaret Sayers Peden's rendition):

Vallejo was shorter than I, thinner, more heavy-bound. He was also more Indian than I, with very dark eyes and a very tall, domed forehead. He had a handsome Inca face, saddened by an air of unmistakable majesty. Vain like all poets, he loved it when people talked to him this way about his Indian features. He would hold his head high to let me admire it and say, "I've got something, haven't I?" And then laugh at himself quietly.

And,

[He] was moody but only on the outside, like a man who had been huddling in the shadow for a long time. He had a solemn nature and his face resembled a rigid, quasi-hieratic mask. But his inner self was something else again. I often saw him (especially when we managed to pry him away from his domineering wife, a tyrannical, proud Frenchwoman who was a concierge's daughter), yes, I saw him jumping up and down happily, like a schoolboy. Later he would slip back into his moroseness and his submission.

While Vallejo's *cholo* self, as well as his interest in the lower-class and the Indian population of Peru, are evident in his oeuvre, Vallejo isn't a poet of *indigenismo* like José María Arguedas, the author of *Los ríos profundos* (Deep Rivers). An anthropologist who studied Quechua culture, Arguedas compiled his country's folktales, and is the other major early-twentieth-century Peruvian man of letters (he died in 1969). *Indigenismo* is an ideology that seeks to represent the rights and beliefs of the indigenous population in the Americas. Even though Arguedas himself emphasized Vallejo's Indian qualities, turning him into a sufferer "who speaks and protests in the name of us all," the truth is that Vallejo's work focuses more on economic issues than on ethnicity. Particularly in his fiction, the emphasis is on class struggle. Interested in Marxism in the late twenties, and infatuated with the Soviet experiment, these stories, Manichean as they are, fall into the mold of Social Realism, asking the reader to sympathize with the oppressed and calling for awareness about the injustice that prevailed in Peru and, by extension, in the entire world. In other words, the troubles of the Inca peoples aren't at center stage.

Although focused on himself, his work is linked to four principal loci: the Andean region; Trujillo and Lima; Paris; and the Spanish landscape during the war. Their impact is felt internally as Vallejo reacts to the environment. What matters to him are people: emotions, ideas, gestures. Between 1905 and 1909, he studied in Huamachuco, where he discovered literature. In 1910, while a peasant revolution, the first of its kind in the twentieth century, known as *la revolución,* broke out in Mexico, Vallejo became a student at the School of Humanities in La Libertad University. But his financial situation, and that of his family, was dire, and he dropped out within the year. Instead, he chose, at least temporarily, what Maxim Gorky called "the university of life": He worked as a miner in Quiruvilca. The following year he moved to the nation's capital, Lima, a city that defined him, intellectually and emotionally. In *Black*

Heralds he described the way it rains in Lima: "the dirty water of a mortiferous, lethal grief." He added, about a love he encountered early on: "It's raining, leaking through the cracks of your love."

Vallejo entered the College of Science in Lima's Universidad Nacional of San Marcos, but again he dropped out because of his financial constraints. He found work as a private tutor for a wealthy family. The encounter with the Peruvian upper class, in the domestic realm as well as in the mines, left a lasting impression on him. The fractured nature of Peruvian society, the remnants of colonialism, and the poverty that surrounded him, made him conscious of the discrepancy between the haves and have-nots. The inspiration for his proletarian novel *Tungsten* dates back to this time. So do his early Marxist readings. But poetry was his passion. Nothing else was of equal importance. At the age of nineteen, Vallejo published his first poem, "*Soneto*" (Sonnet), in the newspaper *El Minero Ilustrado*. (In 2003, Hugo Ariaz Hidalgo and Edmundo Bendezú released a book-long study of it.) Other early poems, also printed in newspapers, belong to this period. He discarded a few as inferior but kept revising a substantial number of them. Later on, as he collected them in *Black Heralds,* they underwent further changes. And so, according to literary historians, already at this stage he devised his editorial method. Publication in a periodical didn't mean the piece had reached its definitive form. On the contrary, as with Walt Whitman, seeing it in print was for Vallejo a first stage on the road to completion. If and when the piece appeared in book form, it was, in his view, as close to finished as possible, although he was notoriously careless about correcting page proofs and both of his volumes of poetry published during his lifetime were plagued with typos and inconsistencies.

The political landscape of Peru in the first decades of the twentieth century, as it is a hundred years later, was colored by inequality. As he worked on a sugar plantation and again enrolled at the School of Humanities in La Libertad University, he was affected by the government's procapitalist policies and by various attempts to organize workers. Those were the years of the first mandate of Augusto B. Leguía y Salcedo (1908–12), in which the oligarchy ratified its place and capitalism was emphasized through the arrival of American capital. Leguía's first period was characterized by economic reforms. He became president through elections. But for his second period (1919–30), known as the *"Oncenio"* (eleventh, in Spanish), he orchestrated a coup d'état. He pushed for a new, more liberal, constitution, but during his time in office he ignored it almost consistently. The tension between the ruling class and Marxist figures became more strident in the twenties, when Leguía drove into exile a number of dissidents, such as Victor Raúl Haya de la Torre, who founded, while in Mexico City, the influential A.P.R.A., the American Popular Revolutionary Alliance, which sought, among other objectives, to create a pan–Latin American socialist movement. The cofounder of A.P.R.A. was the slightly older Antenor Orrego, to whom Vallejo became a close friend in 1914. Years later, Vallejo asked him to write a prologue to *Trilce*. Other young activists were José Eulogio Garrido, Alcides Spelucín, and José Carlos Mariátegui, a political philosopher best known for his book *Seven Interpretative Essays on Peruvian Reality*, published in 1928, who allied himself with Haya de la Torre. Mariátegui was born in 1894, two years after Vallejo, and died in 1930, at the age of thirty-five. Two years before, Vallejo wrote to Mariátegui from France to report that along with some comrades, he had started a Paris chapter of the Peruvian Socialist Party.

Vallejo's early literary readings are equally important. According to Coyné and Juan Espejo Asturrizaga, aside from the *modernistas* he read Whitman, Baudelaire, Verlaine, and Laforgue, among others. He was also quite knowledgeable in the Spanish poets of the sixteenth and seventeenth centuries. In fact, judging from the thesis he eventually wrote, in 1915, to complete his bachelor's degree at La Libertad University, called *El Romanticismo en la poesía castellana* (Romanticism in Spanish poetry), his knowledge of the Spanish-language poetry of José de Esponceda and Gaspar Núñez de Arce was as deep as it was complex, and probably more significant than those of Francisco de Quevedo and Luis de Góngora. He also established connections with important Peruvian intellectuals, such as Manuel González Prada, the director of the National Library (he died in 1918), who became his mentor; ("Eternal Dice" is dedicated to him, for his "savage and select emotion"); José María Eguren; and Abraham Valdelomar. Around then, as Vallejo was seeking to establish himself in the capital while keeping in touch with his family, his brother Miguel died in Vallejo's hometown, Santiago de Chuco. Deeply affected by the event, the poet wrote a eulogy that, after several permutations, became *"A mi hermano Miguel,"* part of *Black Heralds*. It's a poem of extraordinary power, conveying the spirit of childhood through the game of hide-and-seek while struggling to contain the pain that comes when one of our beloved dies suddenly:

> Brother, I'm sitting on the bench at our house
> where your absence is a bottomless pit.
> I remember that this is the time we used to play,
> and that Mamá would pat us and say, "Boys, boys . . ."
>
> Now I'm hiding, as I used to,
> from all those eventide prayers,
> and hoping you don't stumble upon me.
> Through the sala, the entry hall, the corridors.
> Later, you go hide, and I don't find you.
> I remember that we made each other cry,
> brother, playing that game.
>
> Miguel, you hid
> one night in August, near dawn;
> but instead of laughing as you hid, you were sad.
> And your twin heart from those bygone
> afternoons is weary from not finding you. And now
> a shadow is falling over my soul.
>
> Listen, brother, don't wait too long to come out.
> All right? You might upset Mamá.

The poem belongs to the section "Songs of the Hearth," one of the six into which *Black Heralds* is divided and the one concentrating on domestic matters. (The other sections are "Agile Soffits," "Deep Sea Divers," "Of the Earth," "Imperial Nostalgias," "Thunder," and "Songs of the Hearth.") The volume, called in Spanish *Los heraldos negros,* was published in Lima on July 23, 1918. Vallejo paid for the edition himself. Valdelomar was going to write a preface to the volume but fell ill and died before he could do so. The event delayed publication of the volume, but allowed Vallejo to add a few poems.

In 1963, Thomas Merton, in his book *Emblems of a Season of Fury,* wrote: "At times [Vallejo] recalls Rimbaud and Baudelaire, but . . . [he] is more reserved and austere, and, simultaneously, more virile and humble." Elsewhere, Merton stated that Vallejo "is the greatest Catholic poet since Dante—and by Catholic I mean universal." Indeed, a key to understanding Vallejo in general, and especially his first collection, is his Catholicism. His attitude toward it is nothing if not ambivalent. He's critical of the Church as an institution, but he also takes from religion the quest for salvation, which sometimes is presented as a political quest for utopian remedies and at other times results in the application of poetry to explain the schism at the core of his existence. For instance, he questions God but his skepticism cannot push him too far away from Him. The poem "Espergesia," also in "Songs of the Hearth," starts with these stanzas in which he reflects on the abyss that defines his nature:

> I was born on a day
> that God was ill.

> Everyone knows that I am alive,
> that I am bad, but they don't know
> about the December of that January.
> For I was born on a day
> that God was ill.

> There is a void
> in my metaphysical air
> that no one is to touch:
> the cloister of a silence
> that spoke at the edge of fire.
> I was born on a day
> that God was ill.

And in the poem entitled "God," part of the section "Thunder," Vallejo writes:

> I sense God, who walks so deep
> within me, with the twilight, and with the sea.
> With him, we go together. It's growing dark.
> With him, we arrive as night falls. Orphaned . . .
>
> But I sense God. And it seems even
> that he is guiding me to some fine color.
> Welcoming, caring, he is good, but sad;
> a lover's sweet withering disdain;
> oh how his heart must pain him.
>
> Oh, God, only recently have I come to you,
> today, this evening, I love so strongly; today
> when on the false scales of some breasts
> I weigh and I weep a fragile Creation.
>
> And you, how you will weep . . . you, enamored
> of such an enormous revolving bosom . . .
> I consecrate you, oh, God, because you love so much;
> because you never smile; because your heart
> must always give you great pain.

Perceiving the divine as both benign and disdainful, Vallejo comes to Him with love and is puzzled by His heart, which "must always give [Him] great pain." This depiction, in my eyes, infuses a quality of regret in the poet that is in contrast with Franz Kafka's meditation on the divinity as an absent, remote, relentless, and uncommitted force.

In fact, Vallejo's existential perplexity and Kafka's have more in common. Like the author of *The Trial*, the poet in *Black Heralds* feels alone, distanced from humankind, and opts for silence. No one seems to understand him, no one sympathizes with his plight. Silence, actually, is a leitmotif in Vallejo. "Agape" finds him deprecating, skeptical, deep in thought—silence and death:

> Today no one has come to ask questions;
> nor has anyone asked anything of me this evening.
>
> I haven't seen so much as a cemetery flower
> in a joyful candlelit procession.
> Forgive me, Lord. How little I have died!
>
> This evening everyone, everyone, goes by
> without asking a question or asking anything of me.
>
> And I don't know what they forget and what fits so badly
> in my hands, like something that doesn't belong to me.
>
> I have gone to the gate,
> and I want to yell to everyone:
> If you are missing something, it's here!
>
> Because on all the evenings of this life,
> I don't know what gates will open onto a face,
> and something *other* take possession of my soul.
>
> Today no one has come;
> and today I have died oh so little this afternoon!

Interestingly, Vallejo's image of the gate is eerily reminiscent of Kafka's famous Hasidic story "Before the Law," which is part of *In the Penal Colony* (1919). In it a bystander attempts to go through a door guarded by a doorkeeper, who tells him:

"It is possible but not at present." As the bystander pursues his task, the doorkeeper becomes impatient. "What is it that you still want to know?" he asks. In the end, the bystander is told that the door was meant for him alone and no one else. But it is too late. The doorkeeper says: "Now I am going to close it." Vallejo's poem, of course, isn't a moral parable, although some of his prose poems, written in Paris, do feel like such. In "Agape" the reader is left with the sense of failed achievement. His focus isn't the almighty but society. "Today no one has come," he asserts. And, as a result, "I have died oh so little this afternoon!" Like Kafka, he's after enlightenment. Octavio Paz said of Vallejo:

> [He] had a traditional temperament, in spite of his poetical and political radicalism. He didn't conceive poetry as a sort of religion without God but with miracles and revelations; nor did he make language God-like . . . : he turned it into an interior liturgy. Although he professed an elementary form of scientific inquiry and was an atheist and a materialist, his passions and his words were religious. For him poetry was confession, penitence and communion: a true Eucharist. . . . In his poetry verbs, adjectives and nouns perform a function at once punitive and redemptive: like a crown made of thorns, the nails and swords of sacred imagery, they are the sign of his martyrdom and glory.

Black Heralds, then, is about a man lost in the universe—lost and found. Not surprisingly, it includes powerful poems on love and eroticism, on beauty and the discovery of sex. Some of them are about adolescent encounters while in others the desire for carnal bonding is an allegory for a more sophisticated union. In "Dead Idyll," Vallejo juxtaposes love and food and other natural elements. It starts with the following lines:

> What would my sweet Andean Rita of rushes and capulín cherries be doing at this hour?
> now that Byzantium is asphyxiating me, and my blood
> is drowsing within me like pale cognac.

Where are the hands that contritely
ironed in white afternoons to come;
now, in this rain that dissolves
my desire to live.

What will have become of her flannel skirt? of her
chores? of her footsteps?
of her taste like the May cane that grows here?

The sonnet "Amor" is about love without sex and about sex
without arousal. Again, the Catholic undertones are inescapable:

> Amor, you no longer come to my dead eyes;
> and how my idealist heart weeps for you.
> My chalices all are open, awaiting
> your autumnal hosts and auroral wines.
>
> Amor, divine cross, irrigate my deserts
> with your astral blood that dreams and weeps.
> Amor! You don't come anymore to my dead eyes
> that both fear and long for your dawn lament!
>
> Amor, I don't love you when you are far away
> done up like a merry, painted bacchante
> or a fragile woman with a turned-up nose.
>
> Amor, come without flesh, as Olympian ichor,
> so that I, in the manner of God, may be a man
> who loves and begets without sensual pleasure!

The Latin American poet whose songs of Eros are inter-
nationally known is Neruda, Vallejo's junior by twelve years.
Twenty Love Poems and a Song of Despair, his best-selling
early work, was published in 1924, six years after *Black Her-
alds.* Its content is more lyrical. The poet sings to the cosmos.
He isn't tormented by sin, like Vallejo is, but by longing: the
need to keep and reject his lover. Neruda wasn't into stylistic

innovation the way the Peruvian poet was. His pieces are more conventional. This might explain their enduring popularity.

The theme of love, of course, isn't exclusive to *Black Heralds*; it appears prominently in *Trilce* and, less emphatically, in *Human Poems*. On this matter, it is important to reflect on the role women played in Vallejo's life and career. About half a dozen female figures accompanied him in different periods, allowing him to discover unknown parts of himself and, after his death, keeping his legacy alive. First comes his mother, who died of angina in 1918. He writes about her in "Songs of the Hearth": "My mother, like a Lady of Sorrows, comes and goes." And "She is now so mild and gentle, so wing, so Way Out, so love." Throughout his career, the symbol of the mother will mutate: Vallejo will refer it to his mother, to Peru and Spain, and to nature. Then there is Zoila Rosa Cuadra (he called her "Mirtho"). Vallejo had an affair with her from July to December 1917, when she was fifteen years old. Some of the poems in *Black Heralds,* such as "White Primer," might be inspired by her. When the affair came to an end, Vallejo became depressed to such an extent that he tried shooting himself. But, according to Espejo Asturrizaga, the gun he used had only one bullet, and one was obviously not enough.

In October 1918, he began a relationship with Otila Villanueva, the sister-in-law of a Colegio Barros colleague, which lasted until August 1920. Several critics are convinced that the love poems in *Trilce* are inspired by her. The relationship was scandalous. It ended dramatically when Vallejo, who refused to marry Otila, fist-fought with her brother-in-law. Apparently, there might have been an unplanned pregnancy, as Poem X of *Trilce* suggests:

> The pristine and final stone of unfounded
> good fortune, just died
> soul and all, October bedroom and pregnant.
> After three months of absent and ten of sweet.
> How destiny,
> mitered monodactyl, is laughing.

How behind meetings of opposites
all hope is lost. How ciphers forever peer
from beneath the line of every avatar.

These two women, Zoila and Otila, allowed Vallejo to dis-
cover his pleasures of eroticism. In *Trilce* XIII he uses language
to explore the routes of physical pleasure and the connection
between sound and silence, life and death, and the limits of
passion:

I'm thinking about your sex.
The heart simplified, I'm thinking about your sex,
before the ripe childing of the day.
I finger the bud of happiness, it's in season.
And an aging sentiment dies
degenerated into common sense.

I'm thinking about your sex, furrow more prolific
and harmonious than the womb of Shadow,
though Death conceive and give birth
by way of God himself.
Oh, Conscience,
I think, yes, of the unfettered brute
who takes his pleasure where he wants, where he can.

O scandal of twilight honey.
O mute hullabaloo.

Oolaballuhetumo!

Two other women in Vallejo's life were María Rosa Sandoval
and Henriette Maisse. He met the latter in May 1926 and they
lived together in Paris in the Hôtel de Richelieu. Her relevance
is fairly insignificant in comparison to the last female figure,
who was arguably the most important, in his life. Georgette
de Phillipart was the eighteen-year-old daughter of a French
concierge. She lived across the street from the Hôtel Richelieu
when the poet lived there with Henriette, and he first noticed

her while she was sewing. Since he used to make gestures to her from across the street, she thought he was a deaf mute. Later, when she heard him speak, Georgette told her mother that the neighbor could speak! Georgette had a possessive personality. After Vallejo died, she became the keeper of his memory, safeguarding the estate and controlling everything related to him. Along with the Peruvian historian Raúl Porras Barrenechea, who helped him when, in the final moments of his life, a series of medical studies were done to diagnose his illness, she took care of publishing two collections and even chose their respective titles (although Georgette would later on regret the choice of the former): *Human Poems* (in Spanish, *Poemas humanos*), released in Paris in 1939; and *Spain, Take This Chalice from Me* (*España, aparta de mí este cáliz*), in Mexico in 1940. She moved to Lima in 1951, where she continued to promote Vallejo's oeuvre.

Would Vallejo have been canonized as *uno de los grandes*, a magisterial Spanish-language poet, had he not written *Trilce*? In its unsettling of the language, the volume is a parting of waters. It was another self-published book that appeared in October 1922 under the aegis of Talleres de la Penitenciaría in Lima for 150 soles. Several of the poems had been written in 1919 while he was living in Trujillo working as an elementary schoolteacher at the Colegio Nacional de Guadalupe. The last two poems in the *Trilce* anthology, out of a total of seventy-seven, were composed in 1922. He also wrote a handful in jail where he was held as a result of his activism. From Trujillo he traveled to his hometown and had the intention of moving to Lima. He passed through Huamachuco to see a brother of his who was a judge (according to Coyné, in Huamachuco Vallejo announced that one day he would be as famous as Rubén Darío) when, in 1920, he was part of a political riot that took place in Santiago de Chuco that left one person dead, government buildings vandalized, and an important business, property of Carlos Santa María, set on fire. After his attempted escape and while staying at Antenor Orrego's house near Trujillo, the Santa María family pressed charges against him and more than a dozen others and he was imprisoned.

The etymology of the title word *Trilce* is surrounded by myth. It was originally called *Cráneos de bronce* (Bronze Crania). Vallejo changed it at an advanced editorial stage, when pages had already been done. The author was meant to be listed as César Perú. According to Espejo Asturrizaga, in *César Vallejo: Itinerario del hombre, 1892–1923,* Vallejo's friends persuaded him not to use a nom de plume. The title comes from his repeating the word *tres,* three, a number playing an important role in the poems, several times: *tres, tres tres;* and then *tressss, trissss, triesss, tril, trilsss,* until he stumbled upon *trilce.* Another account suggests that *trilce,* a meaningless word in Spanish, comes from a lexicographic combination, a portmanteau, of *triste,* sad, and *dulce,* sweet, a mixed emotion he surely experienced in prison. Indeed, some of the poems in *Trilce* have a suffocating quality to them. The poet seems not only alone and detached but his usual introspection reaches even further. Irish poet Michael Smith argues insightfully that at this point in his life "the notion of temporal and spatial constriction becomes in Vallejo's poetry a link with the inevitability of death, but also with the confinement imposed on the poet by consciousness and language."

In any case, the volume's reception was tepid: No one seemed to care about the book. Or else, it was attacked by people like Luis Alberto Sánchez, who called it "incomprehensible and outlandish." Vallejo was dismayed but he was confident that the content was a harbinger of things to come and that history would vindicate him. In an often-quoted letter that is read as a manifesto, he wrote (in Michael Smith's translation):

The book has fallen into a total void. I am responsible for the book. I assume complete responsibility for its aesthetics. Today, perhaps more than ever, I sense an until-now unknown and sacred obligation gravitating over me as a man and as an artist: to be free! If I am not free today, I never will be. I feel the arch of my forehead swell with its most imperious curve of heroism. I give myself over to the freest form that I can, and this is my greatest artistic harvest. God alone knows the degree to which my freedom is certain and true! . . . I want to be free, no matter what sacrifices I must make. In being free, I sometimes feel surrounded by the most frightening ridicule, like a child who mistakenly lifts his spoon up to his nose.

The innovations of *Trilce* are manifold. Vallejo doesn't compose lineal, accessible poetry. His objective is to stretch language to its limits. To that effect, he fractures spelling and undermines syntax. He coins terms, and places words geometrically, or uses numbers instead of words. Chronological time isn't respected either. Add to this spirit of experimentation the fact that Vallejo wasn't in charge of the edition but left it in the hands of his friend Francisco Xandóval, and the result is a miscellany of avant-garde efforts mixed with non sequiturs and—why not?—deliberate pranks on the reader.

In 1923 Vallejo moved to Paris, with a lawsuit against him based on property damages still pending. Although he contemplated the possibility of returning to his native country, he never did. France, and its capital especially, was for Latin American writers of the first half of the twentieth century *el ombligo del mundo,* the world's navel. In his *Memoirs,* Neruda wrote: "Paris, France, Europe, for us small-town Bohemians from South America, consisted of a stretch of two hundred meters and a couple of street corners: Montparnasse, La Rotonde, La Dôme, La Coupole, and three or four other cafés. . . ." Vallejo's connection to Paris was, once again, ambivalent: He loved it but never quite felt at home, always longing for his Peru. In other words, he was in exile, nurturing a feeling of displacement, what Cortázar later called the sensation of *no estar del todo,* not being quite there. The poem "Paris, October 1936" is an evocation of his place—dislocated, ghostly—in the French capital:

> Of all this I am the only one departing.
> From this bench I am leaving, from my trousers,
> from my grand situation, from my actions,
> from my number split wide apart,
> of all this I am the only one departing.

From the Champs Elysées or at the turning
of the strange little la Lune alleyway,
my demise is leaving, my cradle departing,
and, surrounded with people, alone, unattached,
my human semblance turns
and dispatches its shadows one by one.

And I move away from it all, because everything
is staying behind to provide the alibi:
my shoe, its eyelet, also its mud
and even the bend at the elbow
of my own buttoned up shirt.

The city's magnet, by the way, continued unabated for Latin Americans at least until the sixties. Vallejo felt its allure, as did the authors of "El Boom," the movement that came about in the sixties and included Gabriel García Márquez, Julio Cortázar, Mario Vargas Llosa, and others. Many of them lived for extended periods of time in the French capital.

Human Poems, in Spanish, *Poemas humanos* (the loose title has been the subject of debate), brings together an array of pieces Vallejo worked on at various points in Paris between 1923 and 1938. The original edition included a total of eighty-nine, but various editors have added other poems to reach almost a hundred. It appears that the other two possible titles for the collection were *Nómina de huesos* (Bone Nomenclature, with biblical undertones from Ezekiel 37:1–12) and *Arsenal de trabajo* (Arsenal of Labor). And there have been different labels and groupings for these poems, including *Paris Poems, Sermon on Barbarism* (after a line in the poem "Sermon on Death"), and *Posthumous Poems*. Since the material was left unfinished, all these are merely speculative. The volume includes almost twenty prose poems as well as the Spanish Civil War cycle. Some of these poems were left in a more advanced stage than others. There are disagreements among editors about how to organize them. Some are dated but there's the question of whether the date reflects the time they were written, when they were revised, or another moment when the poet worked on them. Of a handful there are also different versions, written on two or three typewriters. Vallejo could collapse two poems into one or else transform a prose piece into a poem. What we have, in other words, is a notebook with material in different stages of composition. (The poem "Trilce" that opens the section in this anthology was published in the fall of 1923, and, while sharing the name, doesn't belong to *Trilce*. And there's a debate on why Vallejo exiled it from the Madrid edition, too.)

In my view, the collection features some of Vallejo's most beautifully distilled poetry. The poet's materialist philosophy is palpable but so is his Christianity. Striving for universality, the poems explore social, historical, and personal themes. Vallejo is more straightforward than in *Trilce*, less acrobatic as a stylist. Even when these poems aren't quite finished, the result is far more moving: the poet seems to look at himself in the mirror and wonder: who am I? He reflects on his own condition—and his suffering. Here's the opening of "I Am Going to Talk About Hope":

> I do not suffer this pain as César Vallejo. I don't hurt now as an artist, as a man, or even a simple living being. I don't suffer this pain as a Catholic, a Muslim, or an atheist. Today I simply suffer. If I weren't named César Vallejo, I would suffer the same pain. If I weren't an artist, I would still suffer. If I weren't a man or even a living being, yes, I would suffer it. If I weren't a Catholic, an atheist, or a Muslim, I would suffer just the same. Today I suffer from a place farther down. Today I simply suffer.

Because of his mixed race and economic difficulties, Vallejo had been interested in class struggles from an early age. Around the time he was writing the pieces in *Human Poems,* Vallejo began reading Marx and felt the magnetic forces of the socioeconomic experiment in Russia. Full of fervor, he visited the U.S.S.R. for the first time, cementing his Communist political views. When he returned for the second time, he met Vladimir Mayakovsky and visited Lenin's tomb. The result was an outburst of pamphleteer writing. His reportage of the trip, first serialized in Madrid's periodical *Bolívar*, was published in book form as *Rusia en 1931: reflexiones al pie del Kremlin* (Russia in 1931: Reflections at the Kremlin). Vallejo was then invited to the International Writers' Congress in Moscow. Upon his return, he wrote another book about the U.S.S.R. called *Rusia ante el Segundo Plan Quinquenal* (Russia Before the Second Five-Year Plan) but couldn't get it published. There was also fiction and theater. Almost all of it is utterly unreadable today. He fell prey to the Soviet rhetoric of the time, abandoning literature as an expression of human change to embrace a didactic, prescriptive rhetoric that sermonized its reader.

Fortunately, Vallejo's poetry didn't endure such trivialization. According to Coyné, in the midthirties Vallejo had almost totally abandoned the writing of poetry. The muse of poetic inspiration returned to him shortly before the Spanish Civil War broke out in July 1936. The electoral triumph of the left had rejuvenated him but he was appalled by the military reaction. He followed the events closely. He traveled to Spain, visiting Madrid and Barcelona. Between 1936 and 1938, he collaborated on the bulletin *Nuestra España* until Neruda's power over the editorial board left him disenfranchised. He was part of the Second International Writers' Congress for the Defense of Culture in Valencia and also Madrid. His poems were anything but doctrinaire. In fact, as far as poetic reactions to the war go, in my estimation they are among the most compelling written by a foreigner. Some of the poems are a reaction to concrete battles while others seek to reach beyond their context. They have an immediacy and urgency absent from anything else he wrote. For instance, "Mass," at once measured and passionate, uses the image of a dead soldier as a symbol for redemption, suggesting that only when people come together will the massacres stop. According to some critics, its source is a section in Vallejo's *Rusia ante el Segundo Plan Quinquenal,* where he celebrates the "revolutionary masses of historical materialism . . . that only hear the hammering in the factories and the motors in the trucks, day and night." Likewise, "Spain,

Take This Chalice from Me," a call to children everywhere, is a cautionary tale that makes Spain an emblem of universal justice. (The title is a reference to Jesus' words in Gethsemane in Matthew 26:39.) This is one of my own favorite Vallejo poems. It oscillates between outrage and disbelief:

> Children of the world,
> if Spain falls—I mean, you hear that said—
> if her arm,
> her forearm, falls from the heavens, caught
> in a halter lead between two terrestrial plates;
> children, how old the age of sunken temples!
> how early in the sun what I was telling you!
> how soon in your breast the ancient noise!
> how old your 2 in the notebook!
>
> Children of the world, Mother Spain
> is here with the burden of her womb;
> our teacher is here with her ferules,
> mother and teacher is here,
> cross and wood, for she gave you height,
> vertigo and division and sums, children;
> she is with herself, judgment fathers!
>
> If she falls—I mean, you hear that said—if Spain
> falls down from the Earth,
> children, how you will stop growing!
> How the year will chastise the month!
> How your teeth will stay at ten,
> the diphthong in block letters, the medal in tears!
> How the young lamb will still be
> tied by the foot to the large inkwell!
> How you will descend the steps of the alphabet
> to the letter that gave birth to pain!
>
> Children,
> sons of warriors, in the meantime,

speak softly, for at this very moment Spain is distributing
energy among the animal kingdom,
the flowers, the comets, and man.
Speak softly, for she is here
in all her rigor, which is great, not knowing
what to do, and in her hand
is the skull, speaking, it speaks and speaks,
the skull, the one with the braid,
the skull, the one from life!

    Speak softly, I say to you:
speak softly, the song of syllables, the sobbing
of matter and the lesser murmur of the pyramids, and even
that of your temples walking with two stones!
Breathe softly, and if
a forearm falls,
if ferules clatter, if it is night,
if the sky can be held within two terrestrial limbs,
if there is noise in the sound of doors
if I am late,
if you see no one, if you are frightened
by pencils with dull points, if Mother
Spain falls—I mean, you hear that said—
go forth, children of the world; go out to seek her!

The most recurrent word in these stanzas is the cautionary
"if." His call to arms to children, the next generation, to de-
fend Spain brings to mind Neruda's astonishing poem "I Ex-
plain a Few Things." The Chilean poet reminisces of his life in
Madrid's Arguelles neighborhood with poet friends like García
Lorca and Rafael Alberti. Suddenly, destruction takes over—
and what the poet sees are streets filled with children's blood.
"Come and see the blood on the streets," in the end he de-
mands from the reader. "Come and see the blood . . ."

The poems in the Spanish Civil War cycle offer a glimpse of
a different Vallejo: ideologically engaged yet not pamphleteer-
ing, recognizing that his time is up, Vallejo summons his energy

to fire a last salvo. Maybe poetry is power. Maybe it is capable of making things happen. . . .

In March 1938, Vallejo fell ill. His war-related activities had exhausted him. Ever since arriving in Paris, his health had been precarious. In November 1924 he had an operation at the Charité Hospital after suffering an intestinal hemorrhage. At that point he had written to a friend that "there are times, perhaps, more sinister than the very grave. I had never known them before. This hospital has presented them to me, and I will never forget them." But somehow Vallejo bounced back. Fourteen years later it was different, though. He was physically tired. And he felt depressed. His ongoing feeling of alienation had been exacerbated. The left-wing circles didn't welcome him. He had distanced himself from friends like Neruda. And although his reputation as a poet was strong, he felt unworthy because his oeuvre was almost totally unknown, its distribution limited to a small circle of devotees.

Various diagnoses were forthcoming, none offering any concrete information leading to a remedy. He was moved to the Clinique Générale de Chirurgie. Thanks to the efforts of Raúl Porras Barrenechea, a Peruvian historian stationed in Paris, he was transferred to the Villa Arago clinic. He died on April 15, 1938. Since then, a debate has ensued about the cause of death. Was it malaria? Syphilis? (Roberto Bolaño, in his novella *Monsieur Pain,* has Vallejo dying of the hiccups.) Some acquaintances used his general exhaustion to emphasize his martyrdom: The poet, in their view, had died of disappointment with the state of affairs in Spain and in the world at large. Interestingly, it was raining the day he died. His poem "Black Stone on a White Stone," part of *Human Poems,* is a premonition:

> I shall die in Paris when it's pouring rain,
> a day that I already remember.
> I shall die in Paris—and I don't go far—
> maybe a Thursday, like today, in autumn.

It will be Thursday, because today, Thursday, as I am prosing
these lines, my humeri have brought me to my knees
and never, as I did today, have I turned,
with all my road ahead, and seen myself alone.

César Vallejo has died, they all beat him
though he did nothing to them;
they laid it on hard with a stick and hard

also with a rope; witnesses to it are
the Thursdays and the humeri,
the loneliness, the rain, the roads . . .

The poem might be read as proof that long before Vallejo
died physically, he had been preparing himself for it. Or better,
he had been dying spiritually, alone, in silence and slow mo-
tion. A death mask was made on April 16. (It apparently has
disappeared.) He was buried at the Montrouge Cemetery,
but his remains were later transferred to Montparnasse, where
he himself had asked to be laid to rest. His tombstone is next
to Baudelaire's. The mistake on his birth year was corrected
and a line from one of Georgette's poems was inscribed on it:
"*J'ai tant neigé / pour que tu dormes.*"
Upon receiving the news of Vallejo's death, Neruda sent a
eulogy to the periodical *Aurora* in Santiago, Chile. It was pub-
lished on August 1, 1938 (again, in Sayers Peden's rendition):

In Europe, spring is burgeoning over still another unforgettable
friend among the dead: our greatly admired, our greatly beloved
César Vallejo. By this time in Paris he would have had his win-
dow open, that pensive brow of Peruvian stone absorbing the
sounds of France, of the world, of Spain . . . Old warrior of
hope, old friend. Is it possible? And what can we do in this world
to be worthy of your silent, enduring work, of your private, es-
sential growth? In recent years, brother, your body, your soul,
long for American soil, but the flames in Spain held you in
France, where no one was more alien. Because you were the
American specter—Indian-American, as you preferred to say—

of your martyred America, a specter mature in its liberty and its passion. There was something of a mine about you, of a lunar excavation, something earthily profound.

"He rendered homage to his long hunger," Juan Larrea wrote me. Long hunger, it doesn't seem true. Long hunger, long solitude, long leagues of your voyage pondering the question of mankind, of injustice upon this earth, of the cowardice of half of mankind. The tragedy of Spain was gnawing at your soul. That soul already corroded by your own spirit, so stripped, so wounded, by your own asceticism. Every day the tragedy of Spain bored into your boundless virtue. You were a great man, Vallejo. You were private and great, like a glorious palace of subterranean stone with a great, mineral silence and copious essences of time and matter. And deep within, the implacable fire of your spirit, coal and ashes . . .

A toast, great poet; a toast, my brother.

As is often the case with writers misunderstood in life, the period immediately after Vallejo's death was one of intense reconsideration. Aside from the two collections of poetry that Georgette brought out, the first attempt at a *Collected Poems* took place in 1949. Since then, and in spite of the hermeticism of his work, his global reputation has only grown. Still, while his name is famous, he remains one of the least read Latin American poets, in part because of the difficulty in rendering him into other languages. Even in Peru he's far better known than read (the opposite of Darío, who is widely read in Nicaragua). There are libraries, universities, and institutes named after Vallejo. The famous photographic portrait in which he holds his chin with his right hand illustrated the currency bill for ten thousand intis. He has also been featured in numerous works of art, among them the Andy Warhol–like *Cojudos,* by the Peruvian artist E. P. S. Huayco, housed in Lima's Museo de Arte. It is used on the cover of this edition.

If reading Vallejo in Spanish is hard, the daunting task of translating him into another language—especially his *Trilce*—might well be one of the punishments in Dante's inferno. Poets who contain the DNA of a culture are beyond words. "What is translated from Walt Whitman, from Goethe," he once stated in an article, "are philosophical qualities and accents, and very little of their strictly poetic qualities." And he added: "Of them, in foreign languages, one only knows the great ideas, the great animalistic movements, but one does not perceive the great ciphers of the soul, the dark nebulae of life that dwell on a turn of a sentence . . . on the imponderability of the world." Still, Shakespeare's tongue has been rather receptive to him, or at least has attempted to be. Vallejo is a favorite of Sam Shepard, as the playwright reveals in *Cruising Paradise*. His American followers might not be numerous but they are devoted. They include James Wright, Robert Bly, and Clayton Eshleman. For Bly, Vallejo is a poet of "marvelous intensity." He asserts:

> Many poets we all know are able to associate with considerable speed when there are not many mammal emotions around—Wallace Stevens, for example, creates a philosophical calm in his poetry, inside of which he associated quite rapidly—but when anger or anguish enter the poem, they become tongue-tied, or lapse into clichés. Vallejo does just the opposite. Under the pressure of powerful human feelings, of anger, of self-doubt, or compassion, he leaps about widely, each leap throwing him farther into the edges of consciousness, and at the same time deeper into the "depths." As he says, "don't we raise to go down?"

There are approximately a dozen English-language translators of his work, among them Gordon Brotherston, Valentino Gianuzzi, H. R. Hays, John Knoepfle, Kathleen Ross, Richard Schaaf, Rebecca Seiferle, and Michael Smith. Bly and Wright are also responsible for some versions. Yet the most ambitious, and perhaps also the most controversial, of all translations are by Clayton Eshleman, who remains the only one to have rendered *all* of Vallejo's poetry into English in a comprehensive edition published by the University of California Press in 2007. Eshleman sometimes is too liberal in his approach: In order to make the original come alive, he interprets it loosely. Clearly he's more than a translator—he's a reinventor.

Translator's Note

Translate César Vallejo? Well, not exactly. Attempt a translation, yes.

One is aware of the usual problems of the process: culture, lexicon, authors' quirks, historical periods, slang, wordplay, musical, religious, and literary references, among many others. To those, in the case of Vallejo, is added a large quotient of impenetrability. Enigmas that will never be illuminated once the author who created them can no longer be consulted. So from the beginning the translator knows that she will follow a path leading through a text constantly changing from blazing light to most profound shadow. She will feel her way, always searching, always hoping for a ghostly finger to point to one of many possible English definitions for a difficult word, or for a light pat on the shoulder if she thinks she may have taken a leap that lands somewhere near what Vallejo was thinking and feeling as he wrote the line.

I consulted dictionaries, of course. All the standards, plus several devoted to *Peruanismos,* found through the help of colleagues. We are all dependent on them, though they can be the worst of betrayers. Vallejo uses words that have meanings specific to Peru, as well as an occasional sprinkling of Quechua, which I chose to include. They are not vital for a quick reading, though it gives the reader a deeper appreciation of the poem to know that the *corequenque* is a bird whose feathers were worn by Inca sovereigns as a sign of authority; that *huaco* and *huaca* are related in various ways to burial practices, objects, or grounds; that a *yaraví* is a melancholy song; that a *ñandú* is a South American bird, a rhea, similar to an ostrich; and that a *coriconcha* is a temple. It seemed appropriate to leave those words in the poems with specifically Inca flavor. I offer the same argument for having chosen to maintain many words in Spanish, those referring to place, rank, or everyday practices. Even though one wants to move the text into the world of the English-language reader, I find it condescending to anglicize place names, terms of address, and common words that are making their way into our language anyway.

It is reasonably easy to capture the sense of some of Vallejo's lines. Unfortunately those are few and far between. The Vallejo translator must slowly find a way to "read" these poems, to decide how much license to take—for license must be taken—to construct a template on which he or she unconsciously places a poem with the hope of finding similarities of treatment among them, clues to a way to react to the author's implausible leaps and abrupt slashings of flow that mask deeper expression.

One of the fascinations about translating a poem—translating anything, really—is that there is seldom a "correct" solution. Students in translation courses are often upset by that truth until it becomes clear to them that there are simply better and worse ways to move a text into a second language, not one that is definitive—unless, of course, in regard to factual material. Read several translations of the same poem and you will be amused, perhaps confounded, by the differences among them. Translators of Vallejo carry those differences into amazing ranges of interpretation. One example will suffice. In *Trilce* X, relating the death of Vallejo's lover, the last stanza reads (italics mine):

> No hay ni una violencia.
> El paciente incorpórase,
> *y sentado empavona tranquilas misturas.*

Here are four translations of those final lines. First, Michael Smith:

> There is not the slightest violence.
> The patient sits up,
> *and, seated, dips quiet breadcrumbs.*

Clayton Eshleman:

> There's not even any violence.
> The patient rises up,
> *and seated enpeacocks tranquil nosegays.*

Rebecca Seiferle:

> There is not even one constraint.
> The patient sits up
> *and, seated, daubs tranquil mixtures.*

And myself:

> There is not even one violent act.
> The patient stands up,
> *and, seated, paints out tranquil petal showers.*

Extreme variance, yes, but even so these four examples still illustrate the cardinal rule of translation: Somewhere among the many drafts and versions, somewhere deep between the lines, lies the *authentic* poem.

Many writers precede me in translating César Vallejo. I applaud them all, now that I have a taste of what's involved in trying to put on paper something that may approximate the original Vallejo poem. I also have experienced with them the quiet thrill that comes when seemingly intractable words open up to reveal a thought, an image you feared might lie hidden forever. I am specifically grateful to Ilan Stavans, who put up with endless annoyance during the course of my working on these translations. Thanks to *all* those who labor in the Vallejo garden.

—Margaret Sayers Peden

Suggestions for Further Reading

Vallejo's oeuvre has generated much analysis and debate. The following bibliography includes comprehensive as well as partial editions of Vallejo's oeuvre (poetry, fiction, reportage, theater, and journalism). It features significant monographic studies on his work and listings of the various English translations.

Abril, Xavier, ed. *Antología de César Vallejo*. Buenos Aires, Argentina: Editorial Claridad, 1942.

Ballón Aguirre, Enrique, ed. *César Vallejo: Obra poética completa*. Caracas, Venezuela: Biblioteca Ayacucho, 1979.

———, ed. *César Vallejo: Teatro completo*. Lima, Peru: Pontificia Universidad Católica del Peru, 1979.

———, ed. *César Vallejo: Crónicas*. Mexico: Universidad Nacional Autónoma de Mexico, 1984–85.

Benedetti, Mario, ed. *César Vallejo: Masa y otros poemas*. Buenos Aires, Argentina: Espasa Calpe, 1996.

Bly, Robert, ed. *Neruda and Vallejo*. Trans. Robert Bly, John Knoepfle, and James Wright. Boston, Massachusetts: Beacon Press, 1971.

Boyle, Peter, trans. *I Am Going to Speak of Hope: An Anthology of Selected Poems by César Vallejo*. Sydney, Australia: Consulate General of Peru, 1999.

Cabel, Jesús, ed. *César Vallejo: Correspondencia completa*. Lima, Peru: Pontificia Universidad Católica del Perú, 2002.

Cardona-Hine, Alvaro, trans. *César Vallejo: Spain, Let This Cup Pass from Me*. Los Angeles and Fairfax, California: Red Hill Press, 1972.

Coyné, André. *César Vallejo y su obra poética*. Lima, Peru: Editorial Letras Peruanas, 1957.

Dorn, Ed, with Gordon Brotherston, trans. and eds. *César Vallejo: Selected Poems*. Harmondsworth, England: Penguin, 1976.

Eshleman, Clayton, ed. and trans. *César Vallejo: The Complete Poetry*. Bilingual Edition. Foreword by Mario Vargas Llosa. Introduction by Efraín Kristal. Chronology by Stephen M. Hart. Berkeley, California: University of California Press, 2007.

Espejo Asturrizaga, Juan. *César Vallejo: Itinerario del hombre, 1892–1923*. Lima, Peru: Libería Editorial Juan Mejía Baca, 1965.

Ferrari, Américo, ed. *César Vallejo: Obra poética*. Paris, France: ALLCA XX, 1988 reprinted in Mexico D.F., Mexico: Consejo Nacional para la Cultura y las Artes, 1989.

Ferrero, Mario. *César Vallejo: El hombre total*. Santiago, Chile: Editorial Fértil Provincia, 1992.

Flores, Angel, ed. *Aproximaciones a César Vallejo*. 2 volumes. New York: Las Américas Publishing, 1971.

———, ed. *César Vallejo: Síntesis biográfica, bibliografía e índice de poemas*. Mexico: Premiá Editora, 1982.

Fogden, Barry, trans. *The Black Heralds*. East Sussex, England: Allardyce, Barnett, Publishers, 1995.

Franco, Jean. *César Vallejo: The Dialectics of Poetry and Silence*. London: Cambridge University Press, 1976.

Gianuzzi, Valentino, with Michael Smith, trans. *Complete Later Poems, 1923–1938*. Exeter, England: Shearsman, 2005.

González Vigil, Ricardo, ed. *César Vallejo: Novelas y cuentos completos*. Lima, Peru: Banco de Crédito del Perú, 1991; reprinted by Petroperú and Ediciones Copé, 1998.

———, ed. *César Vallejo: Poemas completos*. Lima, Peru: Banco de Crédito del Perú, 1991; reprinted by Petroperú and Ediciones Copé, 1998.

Gradaos, Pedro. *Poéticas y utopías en la poesía de César Vallejo*. Lima, Peru: Pontificia Universidad Católica del Perú, 2004.

Hart, Stephen M. *Religión, política y ciencia en la obra de César Vallejo*. London: Tamesis Books Publishers, 1987.

———, with Jorge Cornejo Polar. *César Vallejo: A Critical Biography of Research*. London: Tamesis Books Publishers, 2002.

Hays, H. R., trans. *Poems of César Vallejo*. New Directions Annual 15. New York: Meridian Books, 1955. Reprinted with an introduction by Louis Hammer. Old Chatham, New York: Sachem Press, 1981.

Hernández Novás, Raúl, ed. *César Vallejo: Poesía completa*. Habana, Cuba: Editorial Arte y Literatura, Casa de las Américas, 1988.

Higgins, James, ed. and trans. *César Vallejo: An Anthology of His Poetry*. Oxford, New York: Permagon Press, 1970.

————. *César Vallejo en su poesía*. Lima, Peru: Seglusa Editores, 1989.

————, ed. and trans. *César Vallejo: A Selection of His Poetry*. Liverpool, England, and Wolfeboro, New Hampshire: F. Cairns, 1987.

Knoepfle, John, with James Wright and Robert Bly, eds. and trans. *César Vallejo: Twenty Poems*. Madison, Minnesota: Sixties Press, 1962.

Lama, Victor de, ed. *César Vallejo: Selección*. Madrid, Spain: Ediciones Envida, 2000.

Larrea, Juan, ed. *César Vallejo: España, aparta de mí este cáliz*. Mexico: Editorial Seneca, 1940; reprinted in expanded edition, with notes by Felipe D. Obarrio and Juan Manuel Obarrio. Madrid: Ediciones de la Torre, 1992.

————. *César Vallejo: Héroe y mártir indo-hispano*. Montevideo, Uruguay: Biblioteca Nacional, 1973.

————, ed. *Poesía completa*. Barcelona, Spain: Barral Editores, 1978.

————. *Al amor de Vallejo*. Valencia, Spain: Pre-Textos, 1980.

Merino, Antonio. *César Vallejo: Narrativa completa*. Madrid: Akal Ediciones, 1996.

————, ed. *César Vallejo: Poesía completa*. Madrid: Akal, 2005.

Mezey, Robert, trans. *César Vallejo. Tungsten*. Foreword by Kevin J. O'Connor. Syracuse, New York: Syracuse University Press, 1988.

Moss, Stanley, ed. *César Vallejo: Trilce*. Trans. Rebecca Seiferle. Riverdale-on-Hudson, New York: Sheep Meadow Press, 1992.

Ortega, Julio, ed. *César Vallejo: Antología*. Lima, Peru: Editorial Universitaria, 1996.

————, ed. *César Vallejo: El escritor y la crítica*. Madrid, Spain: Taurus Ediciones, 1974.

————. *La teoría poética de César Vallejo*. Providence, Rhode Island: Ediciones del Sol, 1986.

————, ed. *César Vallejo: Trilce*. Madrid, Spain: Cátedra, 1991.

Oviedo, José Miguel, ed. *César Vallejo: Antología poética*. Madrid, Spain: Alianza Editorial, 2001.

Podestá, Guido. *César Vallejo: Su estética teatral*. Prologue by Antonio Cornejo Polar. Minneapolis, Minnesota: Institute for the Study of Ideologies and Literature, 1985.

Price, Richard, with Stephen Watts, eds. *César Vallejo: Translations, Transformations, Tributes*. Middlesex, England: Southfields Press, 1998.

Priego, Manuel Miguel de, ed. *César Vallejo: Ensayos y reportajes completos*. Lima, Peru: Pontificia Universidad Católica del Perú, 2002.

Puccinelli, Jorge, ed. *César Vallejo: Desde Europa: crónicas y artículos, 1923–1938*. Lima, Peru: Ediciones Fuente de Cultura Peruana, 1987.

Rowe, William. *Ensayos vallejianos*. Berkeley, California: Centro de Estudios Literarios "Antonio Cornejo Polar" and Latinamericana Editores, 2006.

Sarko, Mary, trans. *Spain, Take This Cup from Me*. Washington, D.C.: Azul Editions, 1995.

Schaaf, Richard, trans. *César Vallejo: Autopsy on Surrealism*. Willimantic, Connecticut: Curbstone, 1982.

———, trans. *César Vallejo: The Mayakovsky Case*. Willimantic, Connecticut: Curbstone, 1982.

Schaaf, Richard, with Kathleen Ross, trans. *The Black Heralds*. Pittsburgh, Pennsylvania: Latin American Literary Review Press, 1990.

Seiferle, Rebecca, trans. *Trilce*. Riverdale-on-Hudson, New York: Sheep Meadow Press, 1992.

———, trans. *The Black Heralds*. Port Townsend, Washington: Copper Canyon Press, 2003.

Sharman, Adam, ed. *The Poetry and Poetics of César Vallejo: The Fourth Angle of the Circle*. Lewiston, New York: Edwin Mellen Press, 1997.

Silva-Santisteban, Ricardo, ed. *César Vallejo: Poesía completa*. Foreword by Salomón Lerner Febres. Lima, Peru: Pontificia Universidad Católica del Perú, 1997.

———, ed. *César Vallejo: Obras esenciales*. Lima, Peru: Pontificia Universidad Católica del Perú, 2004.

Smith, Michael, with Valentino Gianuzzi, eds. and trans. *César Vallejo: Trilce*. Exeter, England: Shearsman, 2005.

———, trans. *Complete Later Poems, 1923–1938*. Exeter, England: Shearsman Books, 2005.

Vallejo, César. *El romanticismo en la poesía castellana*. Lima, Peru: J. Mejia Baca and P. L. Villanueva, 1954; also, *El romanticismo en la poesía castellana*. Facsimile edition. Trujillo, Peru: Instituto de Estudios Vallejianos, Universidad Nacional de Trujillo, 1997.

———. *Obras completas*. CD-ROM. Rosario, Argentina: Ediciones Nueva Hélade, 2001.

Vallejo, Georgette, ed. *César Vallejo*. Introduction by Américo Ferrari. Paris, France: P. Seghers, 1967.

———, ed. *Obra poética completa*. Facsimile edition. Colección Piedra negra sobre piedra blanca. Lima, Peru: Francisco Moncloa Editores, 1968.

Vélez, Julio, with Antonio Merino, ed. *España en César Vallejo.* Madrid, Spain: Editorial Fundamentos, 1984.

———, ed. *Poemas en prosa. Poemas humanos. España, aparta de mí este cáliz.* Madrid, Spain: Cátedra, 1988.

Yurkievich, Saúl. *Fundadores de la nueva poesía latinoamericana: Vallejo, Huidobro, Borges, Neruda, Paz.* Barcelona, Spain: Barral Editores, 1971.

Chronology

1892: César Abraham Vallejo is born on March 16 (there is also a suggestion that he was born on March 7 and his tombstone in the Montrouge Cemetery in Paris erroneously states his birth year as 1893) in Santiago de Chuco, the Libertad district, in the northern Andes mountains. He is the youngest of eleven children. He is raised in a close-knit Catholic family and is encouraged to become a priest.

1900–1908: He attends elementary school in the town and secondary school in the Colegio Nacional de San Nicolás, also in the Libertad district.

1910: He becomes a student at the School of Humanities in Trujillo's La Libertad University. He drops out for financial reasons before the year is over. He works as a miner in Quiruvilca.

1911–12: He enters the College of Science in Lima's Universidad Nacional of San Marcos but again he drops out for financial reasons. He works as a private tutor for a wealthy family. He publishes his first poem, "Soneto" (Sonnet). He then works as a cashier on a sugar plantation, where he witnesses the miserable conditions of workers.

1913–17: Vallejo works as a teacher at the Centro Escolar de Varones and Colegio Nacional de San Juan. He enrolls again in the School of Humanities in La Libertad University. His activity as a poet grows as he writes poems that appear in newspapers. On August 22, 1915, his brother Miguel dies in Santiago de Chuco. Vallejo writes an elegy that becomes "A mi hermano Miguel." He receives a bachelor's degree from La Libertad University with a thesis called *El Romanticismo* *en la poesía castellana* (Romanticism in Spanish poetry), which is later published. After an affair with a teenage girl goes sour, he tries to commit suicide.

1917–23: He lives in Lima, Peru. He continues to work as a teacher at Colegio Barros and Colegio Guadalupe.

1918: On July 23, he publishes *Los heraldos negros* (Black Heralds) in Lima. He pays for the edition himself. His friend Abraham Valdelomar is meant to write a preface to the volume but dies before being able to complete the task. The event delays publication of the volume, which allows Vallejo to add a few poems to the collection. He has an affair with the sister-in-law of a Colegio Barros colleague, who may have given birth to Vallejo's child without his knowledge.

1920: Vallejo is involved in a political riot in Santiago de Chuco after a commercial establishment burns down. Confrontation with the police ensues and there are a number of reported dead. He is indicted along with a handful of others. He escapes but gets caught by the police and is imprisoned in Trujillo Central Jail. He writes poems in prison that will become part of his second book of poetry, *Trilce*. One of his poems receives second prize in a poetry contest.

1921: He is released from jail on bail as a result of pressure from intellectuals, artists, and university administrators. He moves from Trujillo to Lima. He becomes a teacher at the Colegio Nacional de Nuestra Señora de Guadalupe. Vallejo wins the national short story contest for his story "Más allá de la vida y la muerte" (Beyond Life and Death).

1922: Vallejo publishes *Trilce* under the aegis of Talleres Tipográficos de la Penitenciaría. It has a foreword by his mentor Antenor Orrego.

1923: He publishes a collection of stories, *Escalas melografiadas,* and, in quick succession, a novel, *Fabla salvaje* (Savage Language). In June he travels to Paris, France. There is still a lawsuit against him in Peru. He writes some of the poems later included in *Poemas en prosa* (Prose Poems).

1925: He travels to Madrid.

1926: Back in France, with Juan Larrea, who would eventually edit his poetry, Vallejo edits the short-lived avant-garde mag-

azine *Favorables-París-Poema*. He meets Georgette de Philli-
part, who will become his wife.

1928: He visits the U.S.S.R. for the first time, cementing his
Communist political views. Along with some comrades, he
starts a Paris chapter of the Peruvian Socialist Party and by
letter informs the ideologue and activist José Carlos Mariá-
tegui of its existence.

1929: He visits the U.S.S.R. for the second time, where he
meets Vladimir Mayakovsky and visits Lenin's tomb.

1930: Vallejo travels to Spain, where he meets some important
poets, such as Rafael Alberti, Pedro Salinas, and Gerardo
Diego. In December he is expelled from France for his radi-
cal political views.

1931: He publishes a proletarian novel under the title *El tung-
steno* (Tungsten). It reflects his youthful experiences in Peru-
vian mines. His reportage of the trip to the U.S.S.R., first
serialized in Madrid's periodical *Bolívar* as "Un reportaje en
Rusia" (A Reportage in Russia), is published in book form
as *Rusia en 1931: reflexiones al pie del Kremlin* (Russia in
1931: Reflections at the Kremlin). He is invited to the Inter-
national Writers' Congress in Moscow. Upon his return, he
writes another book about the U.S.S.R. called *Rusia ante el
Segundo Plan Quinquenal* (Russia Before the Second Five-
Year Plan) but is unsuccessful in selling it.

1932: Federico García Lorca offers to help Vallejo place one of
his plays on a Madrid stage. Nothing comes of it.

1934–36: He and Georgette get married. He writes two plays,
Colacho hermanos (Colacho Brothers) and *La piedra cansada*
(The Tired Stone). The Spanish Civil War breaks out in July
1936. Vallejo goes to Barcelona and Madrid.

1936–38: Vallejo works as a journalist and publisher for *Nues-
tra España* during the Spanish Civil War. He is part of the
Second International Writers' Congress for the Defense of
Culture in Valencia and Madrid. He writes poems that will
be collected in *Poemas humanos* (Human Poems) and *España,
aparta de mí este cáliz* (Spain, Take This Chalice from Me).

1938: In March, he falls ill. Various diagnoses are offered. He
is moved to the Clinique Générale de Chirurgie. He dies on

April 15. An ongoing debate ensues about the cause of death: exhaustion, malaria, and syphilis are mentioned. He is buried at the Montrouge Cemetery, but his remains will later on be transferred to Montparnasse. Georgette takes charge of his papers, destroying some and editing others.

1939: Vallejo's collection *Poemas humanos* is published posthumously in Paris. In subsequent years other volumes of his work, including *España, aparta de mí este cáliz* (Spain, Take This Chalice from Me) (1940), *El arte y la revolución* (Art and Revolution) (1973), *Contra el secreto profesional* (Against Professional Secrecy) (1972), and his plays (1979), appear.

A Note on the Text

A number of editions in Spanish of Vallejo's collected poems are available, among them by Américo Ferrari and Juan Larrea. However, the two most significant ones are by Ricardo González Vigil (1991) and Ricardo Silva Santisteban (1997). I've consulted them for the purposes of this anthology as well as the critical editions by Julio Vélez (*Poemas en prosa, Poemas humanos,* and *España, aparta de mí este cáliz,* 1988) and Julio Ortega (*Trilce,* 1991). For researchers, I recommend Stephen M. Hart and Jorge Cornejo Polar's *César Vallejo: A Critical Biography of Research* (2002). In English, the most authoritative, if controversial, volume on Vallejo is *The Complete Poetry of César Vallejo* (2007), which has been a valuable resource. It includes a first-rate chronology by Stephen M. Hart; I've made extensive use of it in the preparation of the introduction and chronology of this book. Other biographical sources I relied upon are André Coyné's *César Vallejo y su obra poética* (1957) and Juan Espejo Asturrizaga's *César Vallejo: Itinerario del hombre, 1892–1923* (1965). A heartfelt *gracias* for their editorial comments to Verónica Albin, Rachel S. Edelman, Lauren Fanelli, Isaac Goldemberg, Luis Leal, Eliezer Nowodworski, Gustavo Pérez-Firmat, Elda Rotor, Martín Felipe Yriart, and Miguel-Angel Zapata.

—I. S.

A Note on the Text

"Spain, Take This Chalice from Me" and Other Poems

LOS HERALDOS NEGROS /
BLACK HERALDS

Los heraldos negros

Hay golpes en la vida, tan fuertes . . . Yo no sé!
Golpes como del odio de Dios; como si ante ellos,
la resaca de todo lo sufrido
se empozara en la alma . . . Yo no sé!

Son pocos; pero son . . . Abren zanjas oscuras
en el rostro más fiero y en el lomo más fuerte.
Serán talvez los potros de bárbaros atilas;
o los heraldos negros que nos manda la Muerte.

Son las caídas hondas de los Cristos del alma,
de alguna fe adorable que el Destino blasfema.
Esos golpes sangrientos son las crepitaciones
de algún pan que en la puerta del horno se nos quema.

Y el hombre . . . Pobre . . . pobre! Vuelve los ojos, como
cuando por sobre el hombro nos llama una palmada;
vuelve los ojos locos, y todo lo vivido
se empoza, como charco de culpa, en la mirada.

Hay golpes en la vida, tan fuertes . . . Yo no sé!

Black Heralds

There are blows in life, so formidable . . . I don't know!
Blows as if from God's hatred; as if when struck
the undertow from everything ever suffered
were forming wells in your soul . . . I don't know!

They are few, but they are . . . they open dark gullies
in the fiercest face and strongest back.
Perhaps they are the colts of barbarous Attilas;
or the black heralds sent to us by Death.

They are profound abysses of the Christs of the soul,
of some exalted faith that Destiny blasphemes.
Those blood-soaked blows are crepitations
from bread burning at the oven door.

And man . . . Poor . . . creature! His eyes turn back, as
when someone claps us on the shoulder;
his crazed eyes turn back, and all that he has lived
forms a well, like a pool of guilt, in his gaze.

There are blows in life, so formidable . . . I don't know!

PLAFONES AGILES /
AGILE SOFFITS

Medialuz

He soñado una fuga. Y he soñado
tus encajes dispersos en la alcoba.
A lo largo de un muelle, alguna madre;
y sus quince años dando el seno a una hora.

He soñado una fuga. Un "para siempre"
suspirado en la escala de una proa;
he soñado una madre;
unas frescas matitas de verdura,
y el ajuar constelado de una aurora.

A lo largo de un muelle . . .
Y a lo largo de un cuello que se ahoga!

Half Light

I have dreamed an eloping. And I have dreamed
your laces scattered about the bedroom.
On a dock, farther on, some mother;
and her fifteen years offering her breast at some hour.

I have dreamed an eloping. A "forever"
sighed in a prow anchored in a port of call;
I have dreamed a mother;
a cool green grove,
and the starry trousseau of a dawn.

On a dock, farther on . . .
And farther on, a neck that is drowning.

Ausente

Ausente! La mañana en que me vaya
más lejos de lo lejos, al Misterio,
como siguiendo inevitable raya,
tus pies resbalarán al cementerio.

Ausente! La mañana en que a la playa
del mar de sombra y del callado imperio,
como un pájaro lúgubre me vaya,
será el blanco panteón tu cautiverio.

Se habrá hecho de noche en tus miradas;
y sufrirás, y tomarás entonces
penitentes blancuras laceradas.

Ausente! Y en tus propios sufrimientos
ha de cruzar entre un llorar de bronces
una jauría de remordimientos!

Absent

Absent! The morning when I go
farther than the farthest, to the Mystery,
as if following an inevitable line,
your feet will slip toward the cemetery.

Absent! The morning when like a lugubrious bird
I go to the beach of the sea of shadow
and of the silent empire,
you will be captive in the white pantheon.

It will have become night in your glances;
and you will suffer, and you will receive
penitent white lacerations.

Absent! And in your own sufferings
a wild pack of remorse and regrets
will race past a weeping of bronzes.

BUZOS / DEEP SEA DIVERS

La araña

Es una araña enorme que ya no anda;
una araña incolora, cuyo cuerpo,
una cabeza y un abdomen, sangra.

Hoy la he visto de cerca. Y con qué esfuerzo
hacia todos los flancos
sus pies innumerables alargaba.
Y he pensado en sus ojos invisibles,
los pilotos fatales de la araña.

Es una araña que temblaba fija
en un filo de piedra;
el abdomen a un lado,
y al otro la cabeza.

Con tantos pies la pobre, y aún no puede
resolverse. Y, al verla
atónita en tal trance,
hoy me ha dado qué pena esa viajera.

Es una araña enorme, a quien impide
el abdomen seguir a la cabeza.
Y he pensado en sus ojos
y en sus pies numerosos . . .
¡Y me ha dado qué pena esa viajera!

The Spider

It is a very large spider that will walk no more;
a colorless spider, whose body,
a head and an abdomen, is bleeding.

Today I have looked more closely. Oh how spiritedly
it stretched out its innumerable feet
to every side.
I have thought about its invisible eyes,
the spider's fatal pilots.

It is a spider that trembled transfixed
on a rim of rock;
abdomen on one side,
head on the other.

So many feet and yet the poor creature cannot
resolve its problem. And, having seen it
stupefied in such a crisis,
what pain that traveler has given me today.

It is a very large spider, whose abdomen
is preventing it from following its head.
I have thought about its eyes
and about its numerous feet . . .
And what pain that traveler has given me!

Babel

Dulce hogar sin estilo, fabricado
de un solo golpe y de una sola pieza
de cera tornasol. Y en el hogar
ella daña y arregla; a veces dice:
"El hospicio es bonito; aquí no más!"
¡Y otras veces se pone a llorar!

Babel

Sweet tasteless home, constructed
at a single blow and from a single piece
of iridescent wax. And in the home
she torments and tidies; sometimes she says:
"The poorhouse is pretty; it's right here!"
And other times she breaks into tears.

Romería

Pasamos juntos. El sueño
lame nuestros pies qué dulce;
y todo se desplaza en pálidas
renunciaciones sin dulce.

Pasamos juntos. Las muertas
almas, las que, cual nosotros,
cruzaron por el amor,
con enfermos pasos ópalos,
salen en sus lutos rígidos
y se ondulan en nosotros.

Amada, vamos al borde
frágil de un montón de tierra.
Va en aceite ungida el ala,
y en pureza. Pero un golpe,
al caer yo no sé dónde,
afila de cada lágrima
un diente hostil.

Y un soldado, un gran soldado,
heridas por charreteras,
se anima en la tarde heroica,
y a sus pies muestra entre risas,
como una gualdrapa horrenda,
el cerebro de la Vida.

Pilgrimage

We walk together. Sleep,
so sweetly, licks our feet;
and everything shifts about in pallid
unsugared renunciations.

We walk together. Dead
souls, the ones that, like us,
passed through love,
with sick, opal steps
come out in their severe mourning
and undulate in us.

Beloved, let us go to the fragile
brink of a large mound of earth.
The wing goes in anointed oil,
and in purity. But a blow,
as it falls I don't know where,
hones from each tear
a hostile tooth.

And a soldier, a great soldier,
wounds as epaulets,
takes heart in the heroic afternoon,
and at his feet displays amid laughter,
like a loathsome rag,
the cerebrum of Life.

Pasamos juntos, muy juntos,
invicta Luz, paso enfermo;
pasamos juntos las lilas
mostazas de un cementerio.

We walk together, very close together,
Light victorious, faltering footstep;
we walk together through the lilac
mustards of a cemetery.

DE LA TIERRA / OF THE EARTH

Verano

Verano, ya me voy. Y me dan pena
las manitas sumisas de tus tardes.
Llegas devotamente; llegas viejo;
y ya no encontrarás en mi alma a nadie.

Verano! Y pasarás por mis balcones
con gran rosario de amatistas y oros,
como un obispo triste que llegara
de lejos a buscar y bendecir
los rotos aros de unos muertos novios.

Verano, ya me voy. Allá, en Setiembre
tengo una rosa que te encargo mucho;
la regarás de agua bendita todos
los días de pecado y de sepulcro.

Si a fuerza de llorar el mausoleo,
con luz de fe su mármol aletea,
levanta en alto tu responso, y pide
a Dios que siga para siempre muerta.
Todo ha de ser ya tarde;
y tú no encontrarás en mi alma a nadie.

Ya no llores, Verano! En aquel surco
muere una rosa que renace mucho . . .

Summer

Summer, I am going now. And I am pained by
your submissive little hands in the evenings.
You arrive devoutly; you arrive already old;
and now you will not find anyone in my soul.

Summer! And you will sweep across my balconies
bearing a great rosary of amethysts and golds,
like a sad bishop who comes
from afar to seek and to bless
the useless wedding rings of dead brides and grooms.

Summer, I am going now. Over there, in September,
I have a rose that I leave in your care;
you will sprinkle it with holy water
all the days of sin and sepulcher.

If by dint of weeping, the mausoleum,
with the light of faith, flutters its marble,
raise high your response, and ask
God to keep the light forever dead.
It must all be too late by now;
and you will not find anyone in my soul.

Don't cry, Summer! In that furrow
a rose is dying that frequently revives . . .

Heces

Esta tarde llueve, como nunca; y no
tengo ganas de vivir, corazón.

Esta tarde es dulce. Por qué no ha de ser?
Viste gracia y pena; viste de mujer.

Esta tarde en Lima llueve. Y yo recuerdo
las cavernas crueles de mi ingratitud;
mi bloque de hielo sobre su amapola,
más fuerte que su "No seas así!"

Mis violentas flores negras; y la bárbara
y enorme pedrada; y el trecho glacial.
Y pondrá el silencio de su dignidad
con óleos quemantes el punto final.

Por eso esta tarde, como nunca, voy
con este búho, con este corazón.

Y otras pasan; y viéndome tan triste,
toman un poquito de ti
en la abrupta arruga de mi hondo dolor.

Esta tarde llueve, llueve mucho. ¡Y no
tengo ganas de vivir, corazón!

Dregs

This afternoon it's raining, as never before, and
I have no desire to go on living, my darling.

This afternoon is sweet. Why wouldn't it be?
It's dressed in grace and grief; it's dressed like a woman.

This Lima afternoon it's raining. And I am remembering
the cruel caverns of my ingratitude;
my block of ice upon her poppy,
stronger than her "Don't be like that!"

My violent black flowers, and the barbaric
and vast stoning; and the glacial distance.
And the silence of her dignity
will put the final period with burning oils.

Which is why, this afternoon, as never before,
I am going with this owl, with this heart.

And other women go by; and seeing me so sad
they assume just a little of you
in the abrupt wrinkle of my deep sorrow.

This afternoon it's raining, it's raining a lot. And I have
no desire to go on living, my darling!

Yeso

Silencio. Aquí se ha hecho ya de noche,
ya tras del cementerio se fue el sol;
aquí se está llorando a mil pupilas:
no vuelvas; ya murió mi corazón.
Silencio. Aquí ya todo está vestido
de dolor riguroso; y arde apenas,
como un mal kerosene, esta pasión.

Primavera vendrá. Cantarás "Eva"
desde un minuto horizontal, desde un
hornillo en que arderán los nardos de Eros.
¡Forja allí tu perdón para el poeta,
que ha de dolerme aún,
como clavo que cierra un ataúd!

Mas . . . una noche de lirismo, tu
buen seno, tu mar rojo
se azotará con olas de quince años,
al ver lejos, aviado con recuerdos
mi corsario bajel, mi ingratitud.

Después, tu manzanar, tu labio dándose,
y que se aja por mí por la vez última,
y que muere sangriento de amar mucho,
como un croquis pagano de Jesús.

Amada! Y cantarás;
y ha de vibrar el femenino en mi alma,
como en una enlutada catedral.

White Primer

Silence. Here night has already fallen,
the sun has dipped behind the cemetery;
here it is weeping as if from a thousand eyes:
don't come back; my heart is already dead.
Silence. Here everything is already robed
in rigorous sorrow; and, like bad kerosene,
passion is sputtering, wanly burning.

Spring will come. You will sing "Eva"
from a horizontal minute, from a
gas ring on which tuberoses of Eros will blaze.
Forge in that fire your pardon for the poet,
and it will torment me still,
like the nail that closes a coffin!

But . . . a night of lyricism, your
fine bosom, your red sea
will be whipped by fifteen-year waves
when it sees in the distance, laden with memories,
my corsair ship, my ingratitude.

Afterward, your orchard, your lip offered
and crushed by me for one last time,
dying, bloody from loving so much,
like a pagan sketch of Jesus.

Beloved! And you will sing;
and all that is feminine will vibrate in my soul,
as in a mourning-dark cathedral.

Nostalgias Imperiales

I

En los paisajes de Mansiche labra
imperiales nostalgias el crepúsculo;
y lábrase la raza en mi palabra,
como estrella de sangre a flor de músculo.

El campanario dobla . . . No hay quien abra
la capilla . . . Diríase un opúsculo
bíblico que muriera en la palabra
de asiática emoción de este crepúsculo.

Un poyo con tres potos, es retablo
en que acaban de alzar labios en coro
la eucaristía de una chicha de oro.

Más allá, de los ranchos surge al viento
el humo oliendo a sueño y a establo,
como si se exhumara un firmamento.

III

Como viejos curacas van los bueyes
camino de Trujillo, meditando . . .
Y al hierro de la tarde, fingen reyes
que por muertos dominios van llorando.

Imperial Nostalgias

I

In the countryside around Mansiche
the twilight sculpts imperial nostalgias;
and the race is sculpted in my word,
like a blood star underlying muscle.

From the tower a bell peals . . . There is no one
to open the chapel . . . It could be said that
a biblical tract had died in the word
of this twilight's Asiatic emotion.

A bench with three gourd bowls, a retable
on which a chorus of lips has just elevated
a Eucharist of golden *chicha*.

Farther on, a wind blows smoke from the ranchos
that smells of sleep and of stable,
as if a firmament were being exhumed.

III

Like aged chieftains the oxen plod
along the Trujillo road, meditating . . .
And in the iron of the evening, see themselves as
kings weeping their way through dead domains.

En el muro de pie, pienso en las leyes
que la dicha y la angustia van trocando:
ya en las viudas pupilas de los bueyes
se pudren sueños que no tienen cuándo.

La aldea, ante su paso, se reviste
de un rudo gris, en que un mugir de vaca
se aceita en sueño y emoción de huaca.

Y en el festín del cielo azul yodado
gime en el cáliz de la esquila triste
un viejo corequenque desterrado.

Standing atop the wall, I think about the laws
that are reversing happiness and anguish:
already in the widowed eyes of the oxen
dreams are rotting that have no when.

The village, at their approach, clads itself
in dull gray, in which a cow's lowing
oils into dream and *huaca* emotions.

And in the feast of the iodized blue sky,
in the chalice of a mournful cowbell,
moans an old and exiled *coraquenque*.

Huaco

Yo soy el corequenque ciego
que mira por la lente de una llaga,
y que atado está al Globo,
como a un huaco estupendo que girara.

Yo soy el llama, a quien tan sólo alcanza
la necedad hostil a transquilar
volutas de clarín,
volutas de clarín brillantes de asco
y bronceadas de un viejo yaraví.

Soy el pichón de cóndor desplumado
por latino arcabuz;
y a flor de humanidad floto en los Andes
como un perenne Lázaro de luz.

Yo soy la gracia incaica que se roe
en áureos coricanchas bautizados
de fosfatos de error y de cicuta.
A veces en mis piedras se encabritan
los nervios rotos de un extinto puma.

Un fermento de Sol;
¡levadura de sombra y corazón!

Huaco

I am the blind *corequenque*
that sees through the lens of a wound
and is attached to the Globe
as if to a magnificent revolving *huaco*.

I am the llama, that nothing touches but
the hostile mindlessness of shearing off
clarion curls
clarion curls gleaming with revulsion
and bronzed by a melancholy *yaraví*.

I am the young condor whose feathers
were lost to a Latin harquebus;
and on the fringe of humanity I float in the Andes
like a perennial Lazarus of light.

I am Inca grace eroding
in golden *coricanchas* baptized
with phosphates of error and hemlock.
Sometimes among my stones suddenly prance
the shattered nerves of an extinct puma.

A ferment of Sun;
leavening of shadow and heart!

Idilio muerto

Qué estará haciendo esta hora mi andina y dulce Rita
de junco y capulí;
ahora que me asfixia Bizancio, y que dormita
la sangre, como flojo coñac, dentro de mí.

Dónde estarán sus manos que en actitud contrita
planchaban en las tardes blancuras por venir;
ahora, en esta lluvia que me quita
las ganas de vivir.

Qué será de su falda de franela; de sus
afanes; de su andar;
de su sabor a cañas de Mayo del lugar.

Ha de estarse a la puerta mirando algún celaje,
y al fin dirá temblando: "Qué frío hay . . . Jesús!"
Y llorará en las tejas un pájaro salvaje.

Dead Idyll

What would my sweet Andean Rita of rushes and capulín
    cherries
be doing at this hour?
now that Byzantium is suffocating me, and my blood
is drowsing within me like pale cognac.

Where are the hands that so contritely
ironed in white afternoons to come;
now, in this rain that dissolves
my desire to live.

What will have become of her flannel skirt? of her
chores? of her footsteps?
of her taste like the May cane that grows here?

She must be in the doorway watching the cloudy sky,
and finally, trembling, she will say, "It's so cold . . . Jesus!"
And from the roof tiles, a wild bird's weeping cry.

Agape

Hoy no ha venido nadie a preguntar;
ni me han pedido en esta tarde nada.

No he visto ni una flor de cementerio
en tan alegre procesión de luces.
Perdóname, Señor: qué poco he muerto!

En esta tarde todos, todos pasan
sin preguntarme ni pedirme nada.

Y no sé qué se olvidan y se queda
mal en mis manos, como cosa ajena.

He salido a la puerta,
y me da ganas de gritar a todos:
Si echan de menos algo, aquí se queda!

Porque en todas las tardes de esta vida,
yo no sé con qué puertas dan a un rostro,
y algo ajeno se toma el alma mía.

Hoy no ha venido nadie;
y hoy he muerto qué poco en esta tarde!

Agape

Today no one has come to ask questions;
nor has anyone asked anything of me this evening.

I haven't seen so much as a cemetery flower
in a joyful candlelit procession.
Forgive me, Lord. How little I have died!

This evening everyone, everyone, goes by
without asking a question or asking anything of me.

And I don't know what they forget and what fits so badly
in my hands, like something that doesn't belong to me.

I have gone to the gate.
and I want to yell to everyone:
If you are missing something, it's here!

Because on all the evenings of this life,
I don't know what gates will open onto a face,
and something *other* take possession of my soul.

Today no one has come;
and today I have died oh so little this afternoon!

Rosa blanca

Me siento bien. Ahora
brilla un estoico hielo
en mí.
Me da risa esta soga
rubí
que rechina en mi cuerpo.

Soga sin fin,
como una
voluta
descendente
de
mal . . .
soga sanguínea y zurda
formada de
mil dagas en puntal.

Que vaya así, trenzando
sus rollos de crespón;
y que ate el gato trémulo
del Miedo al nido helado,
al último fogón.

Yo ahora estoy sereno,
con luz.
Y maya en mi Pacífico
un náufrago ataúd.

White Rose

  I feel grand. Now
a stoic ice is glittering
inside me.
It makes me laugh, this ruby-colored
rope
hissing against my body.

  Rope without end,
like a
descending
spiral
of
evil . . .
bloodred, left-handed rope
formed from
a thousand dagger points.

  May it go on like that, twisting
its rolls of crape;
and may it tie the shivering cat
of Fear to the icy nest,
to the last blazing fire.

  Now I am serene,
with light.
And a shipwrecked coffin
is mewing on my Pacific.

El *pan nuestro*

PARA ALEJANDRO GAMBOA

Se bebe el desayuno . . . Húmeda tierra
de cementerio huele a sangre amada.
Ciudad de invierno . . . La mordaz cruzada
de una carreta que arrastrar parece
una emoción de ayuno encadenada!

Se quisiera tocar todas las puertas
y preguntar por no sé quién; y luego
ver a los pobres, y, llorando quedos,
dar pedacitos de pan fresco a todos.
Y saquear a los ricos sus viñedos
con las dos manos santas
que a un golpe de luz
volaron desclavadas de la Cruz!

Pestaña matinal, no os levantéis!
¡El pan nuestro de cada día dánoslo,
Señor . . . !

Todos mis huesos son ajenos;
yo talvez los robé!
Yo vine a darme lo que acaso estuvo
asignado para otro;
y pienso que, si no hubiera nacido,
otro pobre tomara este café!
Yo soy un mal ladrón . . . A dónde iré!

Our Daily Bread

FOR ALEJANDRO GAMBOA

Break-fast is being drunk . . . Wet cemetery
earth smells of beloved blood.
City of winter . . . The mordant passing
of a cart that seems to drag,
enchained, an emotion of fast.

Oh to knock at every door,
and ask for I don't know whom; and then
see the poor and as they quietly weep
give pieces of fresh-baked bread to everyone.
And wrench from the rich their vineyards
with the two blessed hands
that at a flash of light
flew freed from nails from the Cross!

Morning eyelash, do not fly open!
Give us, Señor, our daily
bread . . . !

None of my bones are mine;
it may be that I stole them!
I came to give myself what possibly was
assigned to another;
and I believe that had I not been born,
a different wretch would be drinking this coffee!
I am not a good thief . . . Where shall I go!

Y en esta hora fría, en que la tierra
trasciende a polvo humano y es tan triste,
quisiera yo tocar todas las puertas,
y suplicar a no sé quién, perdón,
y hacerle pedacitos de pan fresco
aquí, en el horno de mi corazón . . . !

And at this frigid hour, when the earth
emits the odor of human dust and is so sad,
I would like to knock at every door,
and beg, I don't know whom, to forgive me,
and bake pieces of bread for him
here, in the oven of my heart . . . !

Retablo

Yo digo para mí: por fin escapo al ruido;
nadie me ve que voy a la nave sagrada.
Altas sombras acuden,
y Darío que pasa con su lira enlutada.

Con paso innumerable sale la dulce Musa,
y a ella van mis ojos, cual polluelos al grano.
La acosan tules de éter y azabaches dormidos,
en tanto sueña el mirlo de la vida en su mano.

Dios mío, eres piadoso, porque diste esta nave,
donde hacen estos brujos azules sus oficios.
Darío de las Américas celestes! Tal ellos se parecen
a ti! Y de tus trenzas fabrican sus cilicios.

Como ánimas que buscan entierros de oro absurdo,
aquellos arciprestes vagos del corazón,
se internan, y aparecen . . . y, hablándonos de lejos,
nos lloran el suicidio monótono de Dios!

Retable

I say to myself: at last I am escaping the noise;
no one sees that I'm going to the sacred nave.
Tall shadows gather,
and Darío goes by with his mourning-draped lyre.

With countless steps the sweet Muse emerges,
and my eyes rush to her, like chicks to grain.
Ether rushes and drowsing titmice pursue her,
meanwhile, the blackbird dreams of life in her hand.

My God, you are merciful because you bestowed the nave
where these blue sorcerers perform their rites.
Darío of the celestial Americas! How much they resemble
you! And from your locks they fashion their hair shirts.

Like wraiths seeking burial plots of absurd gold,
those vagrant archpriests of the heart
drop out of sight, appear . . . and, speaking from afar,
weep to us of the monotonous suicide of God!

Pagana

Ir muriendo y cantando. Y bautizar la sombra
con sangre babilónica de noble gladiador.
Y rubricar los cuneiformes de la áurea alfombra
con la pluma del ruiseñor y la tinta azul del dolor.

La Vida? Hembra proteica. Contemplarla asustada
escaparse en sus velos, infiel, falsa Judith;
verla desde la herida, y asirla en la mirada,
incrustando un capricho de cera en un rubí.

Mosto de Babilonia, Holofernes sin tropas,
en el árbol cristiano yo colgué mi nidal;
la viña redentora negó amor a mis copas;
Judith, la vida aleve, sesgó su cuerpo hostial.

Tal un festín pagano. Y amarla hasta en la muerte,
mientras las venas siembran rojas perlas de mal;
y así volverse al polvo, conquistador sin suerte,
dejando miles de ojos de sangre en el puñal.

Pagan Woman

To go dying and singing. And to baptize the shadow
with the Babylonian blood of a noble gladiator.
And to swirl the cuneiforms of the golden carpet
with the feather of a nightingale and blue ink of grief.

Life? Protean woman. To watch a frightened,
unfaithful, false Judith escape in her veils;
to see her from the wound, and capture her in my gaze,
encrusting a caprice of wax onto a ruby.

Must of Babylonia, unfermented, Holofernes without troops,
in the Christian tree I have hung my nest;
the redemptive vine refused love to my goblets;
Judith, duplicitous life, lay down her sacrificial body.

Like a pagan feast. And to love her even in death,
while her veins sow red pearls of evil;
and thus return to dust, a hapless conqueror,
leaving thousands of eyes of blood on the dagger.

Los dados eternos

PARA MANUEL GONZÁLEZ PRADA,
ESTA EMOCIÓN BRAVÍA Y SELECTA,
UNA DE LAS QUE, CON MÁS ENTUSIASMO,
ME HA APLAUDIDO EL GRAN MAESTRO.

Dios mío, estoy llorando el ser que vivo;
me pesa haber tomádote tu pan;
pero este pobre barro pensativo
no es costra fermentada en tu costado:
tú no tienes Marías que se van!

Dios mío, si tú hubieras sido hombre,
hoy supieras ser Dios;
pero tú, que estuviste siempre bien,
no sientes nada de tu creación.
Y el hombre sí te sufre: el Dios es él!

Hoy que en mis ojos brujos hay candelas,
como en un condenado,
Dios mío, prenderás todas tus velas,
y jugaremos con el viejo dado . . .
Talvez ¡oh jugador! al dar la suerte
del universo todo,
surgirán las ojeras de la Muerte,
como dos ases fúnebres de lodo.

Dios mío, y esta noche sorda, oscura,
ya no podrás jugar, porque la Tierra
es un dado roído y ya redondo
a fuerza de rodar a la aventura,
que no puede parar sino en un hueco,
en el hueco de inmensa sepultura.

Eternal Dice

FOR MANUEL GONZÁLEZ PRADA THIS SAVAGE
AND SELECT EMOTION, ONE OF THOSE FOR
WHICH, WITH MORE ENTHUSIASM, THE
GREAT MAESTRO HAS COMMENDED ME.

Dios mío, I weep for the life I'm living;
I lament having taken your bread from you;
but this poor thinking clay
is not the fermented wound in your side:
you have no Marys who leave you behind!

Dios mío, had you been man,
you would today know how to be God;
but you, who were always fine,
you feel nothing your creation feels.
And man, yes, does suffer you: the God is he!

Since today there are candles in my sorcerer eyes,
as in those of a man condemned,
Dios mío, you will light all your tapers
and we will play with the old die . . .
And maybe, oh gambler, when you play
the luck of the entire universe,
the dark circles beneath Death's eyes will manifest
as two sepulchral snake-eyes of mud.

Dios mío, but this mute, dark, night
you will not be able to play, because the Earth
is a die, its edges worn away, and round
from having rolled so randomly,
powerless to stop anywhere except in a pit,
the pit of an enormous grave.

Lluvia

En Lima . . . En Lima está lloviendo
el agua sucia de un dolor
qué mortífero. Está lloviendo
de la gotera de tu amor.

No te hagas la que está durmiendo,
recuerda de tu trovador;
que yo ya comprendo . . . comprendo
la humana ecuación de tu amor.

Truena en la mística dulzaina
la gema tempestuosa y zaina,
la brujería de tu "sí."

Más, cae, cae el aguacero
al ataúd de mi sendero,
donde me ahueso para ti . . .

Rain

In Lima . . . In Lima it's raining
the dirty water of a
mortiferous grief. It's raining,
leaking through the cracks of your love.

Don't pretend to be the one sleeping,
remember your troubadour;
for now I understand . . . I understand
the human equation of your love.

A tempestuous and treacherous gem
rumbles in the throat of the mystic bombarde,
the witchery of your "yes."

But it's pouring, pouring down
on the coffin of my path,
where love leaves nothing but bones.

Amor

Amor, ya no vuelves a mis ojos muertos;
y cuál mi idealista corazón te llora.
Mis cálices todos aguardan abiertos
tus hostias de otoño y vinos de aurora.

Amor, cruz divina, riega mis desiertos
con tu sangre de astros que sueña y que llora.
¡Amor, ya no vuelves a mis ojos muertos
que temen y ansían tu llanto de aurora!

Amor, no te quiero cuando estás distante
rifado en afeites de alegre bacante,
o en frágil y chata facción de mujer.

Amor, ven sin carne, de un icor que asombre;
y que yo, a manera de Dios, sea el hombre
que ama y engendra sin sensual placer!

Amor

Amor, you no longer come to my dead eyes;
and how my idealist heart weeps for you.
My chalices all are open, awaiting
your autumnal hosts and auroral wines.

Amor, divine cross, irrigate my deserts
with your astral blood that dreams and weeps.
Amor, you no longer come to my dead eyes
that both fear and long for your dawn lament!

Amor, I don't love you when you are far away
raffled off like a merry, painted bacchante
or a fragile woman with turned-up nose.

Amor, come without flesh, as Olympian ichor,
so that I, in the manner of God, may be a man
who loves and begets without sensual pleasure!

Dios

Siento a Dios que camina
tan en mí, con la tarde y con el mar.
Con él nos vamos juntos. Anochece.
Con él anochecemos. Orfandad . . .

Pero yo siento a Dios. Y hasta parece
que él me dicta no sé qué buen color.
Como un hospitalario, es bueno y triste;
mustia un dulce desdén de enamorado:
debe dolerle mucho el corazón.

Oh, Dios mío, recién a ti me llego,
hoy que amo tanto en esta tarde; hoy
que en la falsa balanza de unos senos,
mido y lloro una frágil Creación.

Y tú, cuál llorarás . . . tú, enamorado
de tanto enorme seno girador . . .
Yo te consagro Dios, porque amas tanto;
porque jamás sonríes; porque siempre
debe dolerte mucho el corazón.

God

I sense God, who walks so deep
within me, with the twilight, and with the sea.
With him, we go together. It's growing dark.
With him, we arrive as night falls. Orphaned . . .

But I sense God. And it seems even
that he is guiding me to some better color.
Welcoming, caring, he is good, but sad;
a lover's sweet withered disdain;
oh how his heart must pain him.

Oh, God, only recently have I come to you,
today, this evening, I love so strongly; today
when on the false scales of some breasts
I weigh and I weep a fragile Creation.

And you, how you will weep . . . you, enamored
of such an enormous revolving bosom . . .
I consecrate you, oh God, because you love so much;
because you never smile; because your heart
must always give you great pain.

Unidad

En esta noche mi reloj jadea
junto a la sien oscurecida, como
manzana de revólver que voltea
bajo el gatillo sin hallar el plomo.

La luna blanca, inmóvil, lagrimea
y es un ojo que apunta . . . Y siento cómo
se acuña el gran Misterio en una idea
hostil y ovóidea, en un bermejo plomo.

¡Ah, mano que limita, que amenaza
tras de todas las puertas, y que alienta
en todos los relojes, cede y pasa!

Sobre la araña gris de tu armazón,
otra gran Mano hecha de luz sustenta
un plomo en forma azul de corazón.

Unity

In this dark night my clock is panting
beside my shadowed temple, like the
apple of a revolver that spins
though the trigger doesn't find the bullet.

The white, still, moist-eyed moon,
is an aimed eye . . . And I sense
how the great Mystery is minted in
a hostile, ovoid idea, in a bullet bright red.

Ah, hand that limits, that threatens,
behind every door, and that breathes
in all the clocks, yield and go on by!

Above the gray spider of your skeleton,
another great Hand of light holds
a bullet shaped like a heart of blue.

Los arrieros

Arriero, vas fabulosamente vidriado de sudor.
La hacienda Menocucho
cobra mil sinsabores diarios por la vida.
Las doce. Vamos a la cintura del día.
El sol que duele mucho.

Arriero, con tu poncho colorado te alejas,
saboreando el romance peruano de tu coca.
Y yo desde una hamaca,
desde un siglo de duda,
cavilo tu horizonte, y atisbo lamentado
por zancudos y por el estribillo gentil
y enfermo de una "paca-paca."
Al fin tú llegarás donde debes llegar,
arriero, que, detrás de tu burro santurrón,
te vas . . . .
te vas . . . .

Feliz de ti, en este calor en que se encabritan
todas las ansias y todos los motivos;
cuando el espíritu que anima al cuerpo apenas,
va sin coca, y no atina a cabestrar
su bruto hacia los Andes
oxidentales de la Eternidad.

Muleteers

Muleteer, you are glass-slick with sweat.
The Menocucho hacienda
charges a thousand troubles every day to live.
Twelve o'clock. It's almost the waist of the day.
The oh so painful sun.

Muleteer, you plodded by in your red poncho,
savoring the Peruvian romance with *coca*.
And I, from a hammock,
from a century of doubt
ponder your horizon, and watch, bewailing
the mosquitos and the gentle, sick refrain
of a bad-luck owl, a *pacapaca*.
Finally you will reach the place you must reach,
muleteer, you who behind your sanctimonious burro
fade from sight . . .
fade from sight . . .

Lucky man, in this heat in which all anxieties
and all reasons rear up;
when the spirit that animates the body
can barely move without *coca,* and cannot
lead its beast toward the occidental
Andes of Eternity.

CANCIONES DE HOGAR / SONGS OF THE HEARTH

Encaje de fiebre

Por los cuadros de santos en el muro colgados
mis pupilas arrastran un ay! de anochecer;
y en un temblor de fiebre, con los brazos cruzados,
mi ser recibe vaga visita del Noser.

Una mosca llorona en los muebles cansados
yo no sé qué leyenda fatal quiere verter:
una ilusión de Orientes que fugan asaltados;
un nido azul de alondras que mueren al nacer.

En un sillón antiguo sentado está mi padre.
Como una Dolorosa, entra y sale mi madre.
Y al verlos siento un algo que no quiere partir.

Porque antes de la oblea que es hostia hecha de Ciencia,
está la hostia, oblea hecha de Providencia.
Y la visita nace, me ayuda a bien vivir . . . .

Fevered Lace

Through the paintings of saints hung on the walls
my eyes drag an ay! of night-is-falling
and in a temblor of fever, with arms crossed,
my Being receives a hazy visit from the Notbeing.

A wailing fly on the weary furniture
has some I-don't-know-what fateful tale to tell;
an illusion of Orients assaulted and fleeing,
a blue nest of larks that die as they are born.

My father is sitting in a venerable old chair.
My mother, like a Lady of Sorrows, comes and goes.
And seeing them I feel something that does not want to leave.

Because before the wafer that is a host of Science
is the host, the wafer, of Divine Providence.
And the visit is born and helps me live well . . .

Los pasos lejanos

Mi padre duerme. Su semblante augusto
figura un apacible corazón;
está ahora tan dulce . . .
si hay algo en él de amargo, seré yo.

Hay soledad en el hogar; se reza;
y no hay noticias de los hijos hoy.
Mi padre se despierta, ausculta
la huida a Egipto, el restañante adiós.
Está ahora tan cerca;
si hay algo en él de lejos, seré yo.

Y mi madre pasea allá en los huertos,
saboreando un sabor ya sin sabor.
Está ahora tan suave,
tan ala, tan salida, tan amor.

Hay soledad en el hogar sin bulla,
sin noticias, sin verde, sin niñez.
Y si hay algo quebrado en esta tarde,
y que baja y que cruje,
son dos viejos caminos blancos, curvos.
Por ellos va mi corazón a pie.

Distant Steps

My father is sleeping. His august countenance
speaks of a peaceful heart;
he is now so sweet . . .
if there is bitterness in him, it will be me.

There is loneliness in the house; there is praying;
and there is no news of the children today.
My father wakes, auscultates
the flight into Egypt, the stanching adiós.
He is now so near;
if there is something distant in him, it will be me.

And my mother is walking out there in her gardens
savoring a savor that no longer has savor.
She is now so mild and gentle,
so wing, so Way Out, so love.

There is loneliness in the house, it's too quiet,
no news, no green, no childhood.
And if there is something broken in this afternoon,
something descending, and creaking,
it is two old, white, curving roads.
Down them, my heart travels on foot.

A mi hermano Miguel

IN MEMORIAM

Hermano, hoy estoy en el poyo de la casa,
donde nos haces una falta sin fondo!
Me acuerdo que jugábamos esta hora, y que mamá
nos acariciaba: "Pero, hijos . . ."

Ahora yo me escondo,
como antes, todas estas oraciones
vespertinas, y espero que tú no des conmigo.
Por la sala, el zaguán; los corredores.
Después, te ocultas tú, y yo no doy contigo.
Me acuerdo que nos hacíamos llorar,
hermano, en aquel juego.

Miguel, tú te escondiste
una noche de Agosto, al alborear;
pero, en vez de ocultarte riendo, estabas triste.
Y tu gemelo corazón de esas tardes
extintas se ha aburrido de no encontrarte. Y ya
cae sombra en el alma.

Oye, hermano, no tardes
en salir. Bueno? Puede inquietarse mamá.

To My Brother Miguel

IN MEMORIAM

Brother, I'm sitting on the bench at our house
where your absence is a bottomless pit.
I remember that this is the time we used to play,
and that Mamá would pat us and say, "Boys, boys . . ."

Now I'm hiding, as I used to,
from all those eventide prayers,
and hoping you don't stumble upon me.
Through the sala, the entry hall, the corridors.
Later, you go hide, and I don't find you.
I remember that we made each other cry,
brother, playing that game.

Miguel, you hid
one night in August, near dawn;
but instead of laughing as you hid, you were sad.
And your twin heart from those bygone
afternoons is weary from not finding you. And now
a shadow is falling over my soul.

Listen, brother, don't wait too long to come out.
All right? You might upset Mamá.

Enereida

Mi padre, apenas,
en la mañana pajarina, pone
sus setentiocho años, sus setentiocho
ramos de invierno a solear.
El cementerio de Santiago, untado
en alegre año nuevo, está a la vista.
Cuántas veces sus pasos cortaron hacia él,
y tornaron de algún entierro humilde.

Hoy hace mucho tiempo que mi padre no sale!
Una broma de niños se desbanda.

Otras veces le hablaba a mi madre
de impresiones urbanas, de política;
y hoy, apoyado en su bastón ilustre
que sonara mejor en los años de la Gobernación,
mi padre está desconocido, frágil,
mi padre es una víspera.
Lleva, trae, abstraído, reliquias, cosas,
recuerdos, sugerencias.
La mañana apacible le acompaña
con sus alas blancas de hermana de caridad.

Día eterno es éste, día ingenuo, infante,
coral, oracional;
se corona el tiempo de palomas,
y el futuro se puebla
de caravanas de inmortales rosas.

Januariad

My father, early
in the songbird morning, puts
his seventy-eight years, his seventy-eight
wintry branches, out to sun.
The cemetery in Santiago, anointed
for a happy new year, is in sight.
How many times has he cut a path toward it,
and returned from some humble burial.

Today marks a long time that my father hasn't gone out!
A merriment of young boys scatters.

Other days he talked with my mother
about a sense of the city, about politics;
and today, leaning on his illustrious cane
which rang louder in the years of la Gobernación,
my father is unknown, fragile,
my father is an eve.
He carries, brings, absentminded, relics, things,
memories, suggestions.
The placid morning accompanies him
with its white, sister of charity wings.

An eternal day, this, an ingenuous, infantile,
choral, orational day;
time crowns itself with doves,
and the future is peopled
with caravans of immortal roses.

Padre, aún sigue todo despertando;
es Enero que canta, es tu amor
que resonando va en la Eternidad.
Aún reirás de tus pequeñuelos,
y habrá bulla triunfal en los Vacíos.

Aún será año nuevo. Habrá empanadas;
y yo tendré hambre, cuando toque a misa
en el beato campanario
el buen ciego mélico con quien
departieron mis sílabas escolares y frescas,
mi inocencia rotunda.
Y cuando la mañana llena de gracia,
desde sus senos de tiempo
que son dos renuncias, dos avances de amor
que se tienden y ruegan infinito, eterna vida,
cante, y eche a volar Verbos plurales,
girones de tu ser,
a la borda de sus alas blancas
de hermana de caridad ¡oh, padre mío!

Father, the world is still awakening;
it is January singing, it is your love
resounding throughout Eternity.
You still will be laughing at your little ones,
and there will be a triumphal racket in the Voids.

    It still will be a new year. There will be empanadas;
and I will be hungry, when in the beatified tower
the good melic blind man who took with him
my schoolboy, my fresh syllables,
my rotund innocence,
rings the bell for mass.
And when the morning full of grace,
from its breasts of time,
which are two renunciations, two advances of love
that prostrate themselves and pray for infinite, eternal life,
sings and sends forth a profusion of Words,
shreds of your being,
at the edge of her white sister of charity
wings . . . Oh father mine!

Espergesia

Yo nací un día
que Dios estuvo enfermo.

Todos saben que vivo,
que soy malo; y no saben
del Diciembre de ese Enero.
Pues yo nací un día
que Dios estuvo enfermo.

Hay un vacío
en mi aire metafísico
que nadie ha de palpar:
el claustro de un silencio
que habló a flor de fuego.

Yo nací un día
que Dios estuvo enfermo.

Hermano, escucha, escucha . . . .
Bueno. Y que no me vaya
sin llevar diciembres,
sin dejar eneros.
Pues yo nací un día
que Dios estuvo enfermo.

Todos saben que vivo,
que mastico . . . Y no saben
por qué en mi verso chirrían,

Espergesia

I was born on a day
that God was ill.

Everyone knows that I am alive,
that I am bad, but they don't know
about the December of that January.
For I was born on a day
that God was ill.

There is a void
in my metaphysical air
that no one is to touch:
the cloister of a silence
that spoke at the edge of fire.

I was born on a day
that God was ill.

Brother, hear me, hear me . . .
Good. Now, do not let me leave
without taking Decembers with me,
without leaving Januaries behind.
For I was born on a day
that God was ill.

Everyone knows that I am alive,
that I bite and chew . . . But they don't know
why they hear shrieking in my poem,

oscuro sinsabor de féretro,
luyidos vientos
desenroscados de la Esfinge
preguntona del Desierto.

Todos saben . . . Y no saben
que la Luz es tísica,
y la Sombra gorda . . . .
Y no saben que el Misterio sintetiza . . . .
que él es la joroba
musical y triste que a distancia denuncia
el paso meridiano de las lindes a las Lindes.

Yo nací un día
que Dios estuvo enfermo,
grave.

the dark sorrow of the tomb,
diminishing winds
untangled from around the great riddler,
the Sphinx of the desert.

Everyone knows . . . But they don't know
that Light is tubercular
and Shadow fat . . .
And they don't know that the Mystery synthesizes . . .
that it is the musical
and sorrowful hump that from afar denounces
the meridional step from borders to Borders.

I was born on a day
that God was ill,
gravely.

TRILCE

III

Las personas mayores
¿a qué hora volverán?
Da la seis el ciego Santiago,
y ya está muy oscuro.

Madre dijo que no demoraría.

Aguedita, Nativa, Miguel,
cuidado con ir por ahí, por donde
acaban de pasar gangueando sus memorias
dobladoras penas,
hacia el silencioso corral, y por donde
las gallinas que se están acostando todavía,
se han espantado tanto.
Mejor estemos aquí no más.
Madre dijo que no demoraría.

Ya no tengamos pena. Vamos viendo
los barcos ¡el mío es más bonito de todos!
con los cuales jugamos todo el santo día,
sin pelearnos, como debe de ser:
han quedado en el pozo de agua, listos,
fletados de dulces para mañana.

Aguardemos así, obedientes y sin más
remedio, la vuelta, el desagravio
de los mayores siempre delanteros

III

Those grown-up folks,
whenever will they be back?
Blind Santiago's ringing the six o'clock bells,
and it's already very dark.

Mother said she wouldn't be late.

Aguedita, Nativa, Miguel,
be careful out there, that's where
spirits whining their memories
have just gone by
toward the hushed hen coop, where
the chickens are still settling for the night
after being so spooked.
Better we stay right here.
Mother said she wouldn't be late.

So let's not get upset. Let's keep looking at
the boats—mine is the very best of all!—
we played with them the whole blessed day
without quarreling, the way it should be:
they're still in the pool of water, waiting,
loaded with sweets for tomorrow.

Let's wait here, obedient, no other choice
anyway, for them to come home, the excuses
of those always ahead of everyone grown-ups,

dejándonos en casa a los pequeños,
como si también nosotros
　　　　　　　no pudiésemos partir.

　Aguedita, Nativa, Miguel?
Llamo, busco al tanteo en la oscuridad.
No me vayan a haber dejado solo,
y el único recluso sea yo.

leaving us little ones at home
as if there was some reason
                              we couldn't go too.

    Aguedita? Nativa? Miguel?
I'm calling, I'm trying to find you in the dark.
You can't have gone off and left me alone,
and the only prisoner be me.

X

Prístina y última piedra de infundada
ventura, acaba de morir
con alma y todo, octubre habitación y encinta.
De tres meses de ausente y diez de dulce.
Cómo el destino,
mitrado monodáctilo, ríe.

Cómo detrás desahucian juntas
de contrarios. Cómo siempre asoma el guarismo
bajo la línea de todo avatar.

Cómo escotan las ballenas a palomas.
Cómo a su vez éstas dejan el pico
cubicado en tercera ala.
Cómo arzonamos, cara a monótonas ancas.

Se remolca diez meses hacia la decena,
hacia otro más allá.
Dos quedan por lo menos todavía en pañales.
Y los tres meses de ausencia.
Y los nueve de gestación.

No hay ni una violencia.
El paciente incorpórase
y sentado empavona tranquilas misturas.

X

The pristine and final stone of unfounded
good fortune just died,
soul and all, October bedroom and pregnant.
After three months of absent and ten of sweet.
How destiny,
mitered monodactyl, is laughing.

How behind meetings of opposites
all hope is lost. How ciphers forever peer
from beneath the line of every avatar.

How whales whittle down doves.
How in turn doves leave their beaks
cubed in a third wing.
How we saddle-tree, facing monotonous croups.

Ten months are towed toward a dozen,
toward another farther-on.
Two at least are still in diapers.
And the three months of absence.
And the nine of gestation.

There is not even one violent act.
The patient stands up
and, seated, paints out tranquil petal showers.

XI

He encontrado a una niña
en la calle, y me ha abrazado.
Equis, disertada, quien la halló y la halle,
no la va a recordar.

Esta niña es mi prima. Hoy, al tocarle
el talle, mis manos han entrado en su edad
como en par de mal rebocados sepulcros.
Y por la misma desolación marchóse,
delta al sol tenebloso,
trina entre los dos.

"Me he casado,"
me dice. Cuando lo que hicimos de niños
en casa de la tía difunta.
Se ha casado.
Se ha casado.

Tardes años latitudinales,
qué verdaderas ganas nos ha dado
de jugar a los toros, a las yuntas,
pero todo de engaños, de candor, como fue.

XI

I've run into a girl
in the street, and she's hugged me.
X, discussed, who found her and may find her,
is not going to remember her.

This girl is my cousin. Today as I touched her waist
my hands have crept into her age
as if into two badly new-mouthed sepulchers.
And because of that very desolation she went away,
     delta in the gloomulous sun,
     trine between the two.

     "I got married,"
she tells me. When what we did as children
in our dead aunt's house.
     She got married.
     She got married.

Late latitudinal years,
what strong desires you have given us
to play at bulls, at yokes,
but all of it deception, innocence, as it was.

XIII

Pienso en tu sexo.
Simplificado el corazón, pienso en tu sexo,
ante el hijar maduro del día.
Palpo el botón de dicha, está en sazón.
Y muere un sentimiento antiguo
degenerado en seso.

Pienso en tu sexo, surco más prolífico
y armonioso que el vientre de la Sombra,
aunque la Muerte concibe y pare
de Dios mismo.
Oh Conciencia,
pienso, sí, en el bruto libre
que goza donde quiere, donde puede.

Oh, escándalo de miel de los crepúsculos.
Oh estruendo mudo.

¡Odumodneurtse!

XIII

I'm thinking about your sex.
The heart simplified, I'm thinking about your sex,
before the ripe childing of the day.
I finger the bud of happiness, it's in season.
And an aging sentiment dies
degenerated into common sense.

I'm thinking about your sex, furrow more prolific
and harmonious than the womb of Shadow,
though Death conceive and give birth
by way of God himself.
Oh, Conscience,
I think, yes, of the unfettered brute
who takes his pleasure where he wants, where he can.

O scandal of twilight honey.
O mute hullabaloo.

Oolaballuhetumo!

XIV

Cual mi explicación.
Esto me lacera de tempranía.

Esa manera de caminar por los trapecios.

Esos corajosos brutos como postizos.

Esa goma que pega el azogue al adentro.

Esas posaderas sentadas para arriba.

Ese no puede ser, sido.

Absurdo.

Demencia.

Pero he venido de Trujillo a Lima.
Pero gano un sueldo de cinco soles.

XIV

As for explanation.
This wounds me with earliness.

That way of traveling along trapezes.

Those choleric brutes as if faked.

That gum that glues mercury to insides.

Those buttocks sitting tilted upward.

That cannot be, been.

Absurd.

Dementia.

But I have come from Trujillo to Lima.
But I earn a wage of five *soles*.

XV

En el rincón aquel, donde dormimos juntos
tantas noches, ahora me he sentado
a caminar. La cuja de los novios difuntos
fue sacada, o talvez qué habrá pasado.

Has venido temprano a otros asuntos,
y ya no estás. Es el rincón
donde a tu lado, leí una noche,
entre tus tiernos puntos,
un cuento de Daudet. Es el rincón
amado. No lo equivoques.

Me he puesto a recordar los días
de verano idos, tu entrar y salir,
poca y harta y pálida por los cuartos,

En esta noche pluviosa,
ya lejos de ambos dos, salto de pronto . . .
Son dos puertas abriéndose cerrándose,
dos puertas que al viento van y vienen
sombra   a   sombra.

XV

In that corner, where we slept together
so many nights, I have sat myself down to
take a stroll. The bedstead of the dead bride and groom
has been taken out, or maybe what could have happened.

On other matters you have come early
but aren't here now. It is the corner
where beside you one night I read,
between your tender buds,
a story by Daudet. It is our favorite
corner. Don't mistake it.

I have set my mind to remembering the days
of bygone summers, your coming in, leaving,
small and fed up and pale through all the rooms.

On this rainy night.
now far from both, I suddenly flinch . . .
It is two doors opening closing,
two doors swinging back and forth in the wind
shadow   to   shadow.

XVI

Tengo fe en ser fuerte.
Dame, aire manco, dame ir
galoneándome de ceros a la izquierda.
Y tú, sueño, dame tu diamante implacable,
tu tiempo de deshora.

Tengo fe en ser fuerte.
Por allí avanza cóncava mujer,
cantidad incolora, cuya
gracia se cierra donde me abro.

Al aire, fray pasado. Cangrejos, zote!
Avístase la verde bandera presidencial,
arriando las seis banderas restantes,
todas las colgaduras de la vuelta.

Tengo fe en que soy,
y en que he sido menos.

Ea! Buen primero!

XVI

I have faith in being strong.
Give me, maimed air, give me indulgence
to galloon myself with meaningless braid.
And you, dream, give me your implacable diamond,
your untimely time.

I have faith in being strong.
A concave woman is moving forward there,
a colorless quantity, whose
grace closes where I open.

Up in the air, once friar. Rogues, fool!
Catch a glimpse of the green presidential flag—
all the other six are being struck—
all the bunting of the change.

I have faith that I am,
and that I have been less.

Hoopah! Clever start!

XXIV

Al borde de un sepulcro florecido
transcurren dos marías llorando,
llorando a mares.

El ñandú desplumado del recuerdo
alarga su postrera pluma,
y con ella la mano negativa de Pedro
graba en un domingo de ramos
resonancias de exequias y de piedras.

Del borde de un sepulcro removido
se alejan dos marías contando.

Lunes.

XXIV

Near a flower-strewn sepulcher
pass two weeping Marys,
flooding tears.

The plucked ñandú of memory
trails its last plume,
and with it the negative hand of Peter
scribes on a Palm Sunday
resonances of exequies and stones.

From the front of an opened sepulcher
go two Marys singing.

Monday.

XXVIII

He almorzado solo ahora, y no he tenido
madre, ni súplica, ni sírvete, ni agua,
ni padre que, en el facundo ofertorio
de los choclos, pregunte para su tardanza
de imagen, por los broches mayores del sonido.

Cómo iba yo a almorzar. Cómo me iba a servir
de tales platos distantes esas cosas,
cuando habráse quebrado el propio hogar,
cuando no asoma ni madre a los labios.
Cómo iba yo a almorzar nonada.

A la mesa de un buen amigo he almorzado
con su padre recién llegado del mundo,
con sus canas tías que hablan
en tordillo retinte de porcelana,
bisbiseando por todos sus viudos alvéolos;
y con cubiertos francos de alegres tiroriros,
porque estánse en su casa. Así, qué gracia!
Y me han dolido los cuchillos
de esta mesa en todo el paladar.

El yantar de estas mesas así, en que se prueba
amor ajeno en vez del propio amor,
torna tierra el bocado que no brinda la

        MADRE,
hace golpe la dura deglusión; el dulce,
hiel; aceite funéreo, el café.

XXVIII

Now I have eaten lunch, alone, and have had
no mother, or entreaty, or help yourself, or water,
or father who, in his fluent offertory
of boiled corn, asks about his delay
of image, and for the larger clasps of sound.

How was I going to eat. How was I going to serve myself
those things from such distant plates,
when our very hearth will have been broken,
when not even a glimpse of mother touches my lips.
How was I going to eat a bite.

I have had lunch at the table of a good friend
with his father recently arrived from the world,
with his white-haired aunts chattering
in the dappled chinking of china,
buzzing about all their alveolate widowers;
and generous place settings of joyous tootlings
because they are in his house. Ah, how pleasant!
And the knives of this table
have hurt every bit of my palate.

Thus the victuals of these tables, which demonstrate
altruistic rather than selfish love,
turn to dirt the mouthful not offered by the
                    MOTHER,
make difficult deglutition a blow; the sweet,
bile; coffee, funereal oil.

Cuando ya se ha quebrado el propio hogar,
y el sírvete materno no sale de la
tumba,
la cocina a oscuras, la miseria de amor.

When your own hearth has already been broken,
and the maternal help-yourself does not leave the tomb,
the kitchen in darkness, the misery of love.

XXXIV

Se acabó el extraño, con quien, tarde
la noche, regresabas parla y parla.
Ya no habrá quien me aguarde,
dispuesto mi lugar, bueno lo malo.

Se acabó la calurosa tarde;
tu gran bahía y tu clamor, la charla
con tu madre acabada
que nos brindaba un té lleno de tarde.

Se acabó todo al fin: las vacaciones,
tu obediencia de pechos, tu manera
de pedirme que no me vaya fuera.

Y se acabó el diminutivo, para
mi mayoría en el dolor sin fin,
y nuestro haber nacido así sin causa.

XXXIV

It's ended, the stranger with whom, late in
the night, you came home talking, talking.
Now there won't be anyone waiting for me,
my place ready, the bad good.

It's ended, the warm afternoon;
your large harbor and your wail; ended
the chatting with your mother,
who fixed us tea brimming with afternoon.

It's ended, it's finally over: the holidays,
your obedient breasts, your way
of asking me not to go.

And it's ended, the diminutive, because of
my being of age in the grief without end
and our having been born for no reason.

XXXV

El encuentro con la amada
tánto alguna vez, es un simple detalle,
casi un programa hípico en violado,
que de tan largo no se puede doblar bien.

El almuerzo con ella que estaría
poniendo el plato que nos gustara ayer
y se repite ahora,
pero con algo más de mostaza;
el tenedor absorto, su doneo radiante
de pistilo en mayo, y su verecundia
de a centavito, por quítame allá esa paja.
Y la cerveza lírica y nerviosa
a la que celan sus dos pezones sin lúpulo,
y que no se debe tomar mucho!

Y los demás encantos de la mesa
que aquella núbil campaña borda
con sus propias baterías germinales
que han operado toda la mañana,
según me consta, a mí,
amoroso notario de sus intimidades,
y con las diez varillas mágicas
de sus dedos pancreáticos.

Mujer que, sin pensar en nada más allá,
suelta el mirlo y se pone a conversarnos

XXXV

The meeting with the beloved
once so much, is a simple detail,
nearly a horse-track program in violet,
so long it cannot easily be folded.

Lunch with her who would be
setting out the dish we liked yesterday
and is repeated now,
but with a little more mustard;
the fork in a trance, her radiant quality
of a pistil in May, and her bought on the cheap
modesty, for no reason at all.
And the lyric and nervous beer
watched closely by breasts untouched by hops,
and that you mustn't drink too much!

And the rest of the table's charms
that this nubile campaign embroiders
with her own germinal mechanisms
that have been operating all morning long,
it appears to me, to me
the amorous notary of her intimacies,
and with the ten magical sticks
of her pancreatic fingers.

Woman who, without thinking of anything beyond,
lets her tongue fly and begins our conversation,

sus palabras tiernas
como lancinantes lechugas recién cortadas.

Otro vaso, y me voy. Y nos marchamos,
ahora sí, a trabajar.

Entre tanto, ella se interna
entre los cortinajes y ¡oh aguja de mis días
desgarrados! se sienta a la orilla
de una costura, a coserme el costado
a su costado,
a pegar el botón de esa camisa,
que se ha vuelto a caer. Pero hase visto!

her words as tender
as lacinating lettuces freshly cut.

    One more glass, and I'm going. And we march off,
yes, now, to work.

    In the meantime, she steps
between the curtains and, O needle of my shredded
days! sits at the shore
of some sewing, to sew my side
to her side,
to tightly fasten the shirt button
that has fallen off again. Have you seen such a thing!

XXXVI

Pugnamos ensartarnos por un ojo de aguja,
enfrentados, a las ganadas.
Amoniácase casi el cuarto ángulo del círculo.
¡Hembra se continúa el macho, a raíz
de probables senos, y precisamente
a raíz de cuanto no florece.

¿Por ahí estás, Venus de Milo?
Tú manqueas apenas, pululando
entrañada en los brazos plenarios
de la existencia,
de esta existencia que todaviiza
perenne imperfección.
Venus de Milo, cuyo cercenado, increado
brazo revuélvese y trata de encodarse
a través de verdeantes guijarros gagos,
ortivos nautilos, aunes que gatean
recién, vísperas inmortales.
Laceadora de inminencias, laceadora
del paréntesis.

Rehusad, y vosotros, a posar las plantas
en la seguridad dupla de la Armonía.
Rehusad la simetría a buen seguro.
Intervenid en el conflicto
de puntas que se disputan
en la más torionda de las justas
el salto por el ojo de la aguja!

XXXVI

We struggle to thread ourselves through the eye of a needle,
looking over at the cattle.
The fourth angle of the circle is nearly ammoniated.
Male continues as female because of
probable breasts, and precisely
because of what does not blossom forth!

Are you there, Venus de Milo?
You feign lameness, barely growing new shoots,
buried in the plenary arms
of existence,
of this existence that stillyetizes
perennial imperfection.
Venus de Milo, whose severed, increate arm
turns round and round and tries to elbow itself
across greening, stuttering pebbles,
ortive nautiluses, evens just beginning
to crawl, immortal eves,
Lassoess of imminences, lassoess
of the parenthesis.

Refuse, all of you, to set foot
on the duple security of Harmony.
Refuse symmetry as certainty.
Intervene in the conflict
of disputing parts of the herd
in the most rutting-ready of the jousts
the leap through the eye of the needle!

Tal siento ahora al meñique
demás en la siniestra. Lo veo y creo
no debe serme, o por lo menos que está
en sitio donde no debe.
Y me inspira rabia y me azarea
y no hay cómo salir de él, sino haciendo
la cuenta de que hoy es jueves.

¡Ceded al nuevo impar
      potente de orfandad!

I feel now the useless little
finger on my left hand. I see it and I believe
it must not be me, or at least that it is
in a place it shouldn't be.
And it enrages me and startles me
and there is no how to get out of it, except pretending
that today is Thursday.

Yield to the potent new
      inequality of orphanhood!

LVI

Todos los días amanezco a ciegas
a trabajar para vivir; y tomo el desayuno,
sin probar ni gota de él, todas las mañanas.
Sin saber si he logrado, o más nunca,
algo que brinca del sabor
o es sólo corazón y que ya vuelto, lamentará
hasta dónde esto es lo menos.

El niño crecería ahito de felicidad
        oh albas,
ante el pesar de los padres de no poder dejarnos
de arrancar de sus sueños de amor a este mundo;
ante ellos que, como Dios, de tanto amor
se comprendieron hasta creadores
y nos quisieron hasta hacernos daño.

Flecos de invisible trama,
dientes que huronean desde la neutra emoción,
        pilares
libres de base y coronación,
en la gran boca que ha perdido el habla.

Fósforo y fósforo en la oscuridad,
lágrima y lágrima en la polvareda.

LVI

Every day I awake blindly
to work in order to live; and I eat breakfast,
without tasting a bite of it, every morning.
Never knowing whether I've achieved, more likely, never,
something that frisks with flavor
or is merely heart that now it's back will regret
as far as this is least.

The child would grow glutted with happiness
          oh dawns,
before the grief of parents unable to prevent us
from tearing them from their dreams of love back to this world;
before those who, like God, from so much love
have thought themselves even creators
and loved us to the point of doing harm.

Fraying of invisible woof,
teeth that ferret from neutral emotion,
          pillars
free of foundation and capstone,
in the great mouth that has lost its speech.

Match and match in the darkness,
tear and tear in the dust.

LXV

Madre, me voy mañana a Santiago,
a mojarme en tu bendición y en tu llanto.
Acomodando estoy mis desengaños y el rosado
de llaga de mis falsos trajines.

Me esperará tu arco de asombro,
las tonsuradas columnas de tus ansias
que se acaban la vida. Me esperará el patio,
el corredor de abajo con sus tondos y repulgos
de fiesta. Me esperará mi sillón ayo,
aquel buen quijarudo trasto de dinástico
cuero, que pára no más rezongando a las nalgas
tataranietas, de correa a correhuela.

Estoy cribando mis cariños más puros.
Estoy ejeando ¿no oyes jadear la sonda?
                    ¿no oyes tascar dianas?
estoy plasmando tu fórmula de amor
para todos los huecos de este suelo.
Oh si se dispusieran los tácitos volantes
para todas las cintas más distantes,
para todas las citas más distintas.

Así, muerta inmortal. Así.
Bajo los dobles arcos de tu sangre, por donde
hay que pasar tan de puntillas, que hasta mi padre
para ir por allí,

LXV

Mother, I am going tomorrow to Santiago,
to drench myself in your benediction and your tears.
I am finding a place for my disillusion and the rose-colored
wound of my false busyness.

Your arc of amazement will await me,
the tonsured columns of your yearnings
that bring an end to life. The patio will be waiting,
the downstairs corridor with its moldings and festive
trimmings. My tutor chair will be waiting,
that good lantern-jawed piece of dynastic leather
that accepts, merely groaning, the great-great-
grandchildren's buttocks, from strip to strap.

I am sieving my purest affections.
I am axleing, don't you hear the drill chuffing?
        don't you hear reveilles scutching?
I am shaping your formula of love
for all the holes in this ground.
Oh, if the tacit tracts would prepare themselves
for all the most distant adornments,
for all the most distinct appointments.

So, immortal departed. So.
Beneath the double arcs of your blood, where all
must so quietly tiptoe that even my father,
in order to pass through,

humildóse hasta menos de la mitad del hombre,
hasta ser el primer pequeño que tuviste.

Así, muerta inmortal.
Entre la columnata de tus huesos
que no puede caer ni a lloros,
y a cuyo lado ni el Destino pudo entrometer
ni un solo dedo suyo.

Así, muerta inmortal.
Así.

humbled himself to less than half a man,
to being your first little one.

So, immortal departed.
In the columnal structure of your bones
that not even weeping can topple,
and at whose side not even Destiny could find a chink
to stick a finger in.

So, immortal departed.
So.

POEMAS HUMANOS /
HUMAN POEMS

Trilce

Hay un lugar que yo me sé
en este mundo, nada menos,
adonde nunca llegaremos.

Donde, aun si nuestro pie
llegase a dar por un instante
será, en verdad, como no estarse.

Es ese sitio que se ve
a cada rato en esta vida,
andando, andando de uno en fila.

Más acá de mí mismo y de
mi par de yemas, lo he entrevisto
siempre lejos de los destinos.

Ya podéis iros a pie
o a puro sentimiento en pelo,
que a él no arriban ni los sellos.

El horizonte color té
se muere por colonizarle
para su gran cualquiera parte.

Mas el lugar que yo me sé,
en este mundo, nada menos,
hombreado va con los reversos.

Trilce

There's a place I-me knows
in this world, no less,
that we will never get to.

Where, even if we are able
to set foot for an instant it will,
in truth, be like not being there.

It's that place in which we are seen
from time to time in this life,
walking, walking in single file.

Nearer to me myself, and to
my pair of yolks, I have glimpsed it
always far from destinations.

You can go there now on foot
or by pure, bare sensation,
for not even stamps will get there.

The tea-colored horizon
is dying to colonize it
for its grand anyone spot.

But the place that I-me knows,
in this world, no less,
goes shouldering along its reverses.

-Cerrad aquella puerta que
está entreabierta en las entrañas
de ese espejo. -¿Está? -No; su hermana.

-No se puede cerrar. No se
puede llegar nunca a aquel sitio
do van en rama los pestillos.

Tal es el lugar que yo me sé.

—*1923*

"Close the door that's
standing ajar in the entrails
of that mirror." "It's here . . . ?" "No; its sister."

"It can't be closed. It will never
be possible to reach that place
where latches are not tinkered with."

Such is the place I-me knows.

—*1923*

La violencia de las horas

Todos han muerto.

Murió doña Antonia, la ronca, que hacía pan barato en el burgo.

Murió el cura Santiago, a quien placía le saludasen los jóvenes y las mozas, respondiéndoles a todos, indistintamente: "Buenos días, José! Buenos días, María!"

Murió aquella joven rubia, Carlota, dejando un hijito de meses, que luego también murió, a los ocho días de la madre.

Murió mi tía Albina, que solía cantar tiempos y modos de heredad, en tanto cosía en los corredores, para Isidora, la criada de oficio, la honrosísima mujer.

Murió un viejo tuerto, su nombre no recuerdo, pero dormía al sol de la mañana, sentado ante la puerta del hojalatero de la esquina.

Murió Rayo, el perro de mi altura, herido de un balazo de no se sabe quién.

Murió Lucas, mi cuñado en la paz de las cinturas, de quien me acuerdo cuando llueve y no hay nadie en mi experiencia.

Violence of the Hours

They're all dead.

Doña Antonia, the hoarse one who makes bread for the poor of the town.

The priest Santiago died, who liked the young people of the village to greet him, instantly replying, undiscriminating: "A good day to you, José! A good day to you, María!"

That young blond girl, Carlota, died, leaving an infant of only a few months, who then died a week after its mother.

My aunt Albina died, who liked to sing of old times and country ways while she sewed in the corridors, for Isidora, the servant by trade, a most honorable woman.

A one-eyed old man died, I don't remember his name, but he dozed in the morning sun, sitting in front of the door of the corner tin shop.

Rayo died, a dog as tall as I am, shot by a bullet from no one knows who.

Lucas died, my brother-in-law in the peace of tight cinches, whom I remember when it rains and there is no one in my experience.

Murió en mi revólver mi madre, en mi puño mi hermana y mi hermano en mi víscera sangrienta, los tres ligados por un género triste de tristeza, en el mes de agosto de años sucesivos.

Murió el músico Méndez, alto y muy borracho, que solfeaba en su clarinete tocatas melancólicas, a cuyo articulado se dormían las gallinas de mi barrio, mucho antes de que el sol se fuese.

Murió mi eternidad y estoy velándola.

—1924

My mother died in my revolver, my sister in my fist, and my brother in my bleeding gut, the three bound together by a sad kind of sadness, in the month of August of successive years.

The musician Méndez died, tall and very drunk, who solfaed melancholy toccatas on his clarinet, at which articulation all the hens in my barrio slept, long before the sun set.

My eternity died and I am mourning at its wake.

—1924

Las ventanas se han estremecido, elaborando una metafísica del universo. Vidrios han caído. Un enfermo lanza su queja: la mitad por su boca lenguada y sobrante, y toda entera, por el ano de su espalda.

Es el huracán. Un castaño del jardín de las Tullerías habráse abatido, al soplo del viento, que mide ochenta metros por segundo. Capiteles de los barrios antiguos, habrán caído, hendiendo, matando.

¿De qué punto, interrogo, oyendo a ambas riberas de los océanos, de qué punto viene este huracán, tan digno de crédito, tan honrado de deuda, derecho a las ventanas del hospital? ¡Ay! las direcciones inmutables, que oscilan entre el huracán y esta pena directa de toser o defecar! ¡Ay! las direcciones inmutables, que así prenden muerte en las entrañas del hospital y despiertan células clandestinas, a deshora, en los cadáveres.

¿Qué pensaría de sí el enfermo de enfrente, ése que está durmiendo, si hubiera percibido el huracán? El pobre duerme, boca arriba, a la cabeza de su morfina, a los pies de toda su cordura. Un adarme más o menos en la dosis y le llevarán a enterrar, el vientre roto, la boca arriba, sordo al huracán, sordo a su vientre roto, ante el cual suelen los médicos dialogar y cavilar largamente, para, al fin, pronunciar sus llanas palabras de hombres.

The Windows Have Shuddered . . .

The windows have shuddered, elaborating a metaphysic of the universe. Glass has fallen. A sick man looses his moan: half by way of his swollen-tongued and superfluous mouth and the whole of it by way of the anus in his back.

It is the hurricane. A chestnut tree in the Tuilleries will have been felled by the breath of the wind, which measures eight meters per second. Capitals in the old barrios will have fallen, splintering, killing.

From where, I ask, hearing both shores of the oceans, from where does this hurricane, so deserving of credit, so honorable with debt, head straight for the hospital windows? Ay! Immutable directions, which swing between the hurricane and this direct pain of coughing or defecating! Ay! Immutable directions, which in that way trap death in the innards of the hospital and awaken clandestine cells, inopportunely, in the corpses.

What would the sick man across the aisle, the one who's sleeping, think of himself if he had sensed the hurricane? The poor man is on his back, sleeping, at the head of his morphine, at the feet of all his good sense. One drop more or less in the dosage and they will carry him off to be buried, gut ruptured, on his back, deaf to the hurricane, deaf to his ruptured belly, over which the doctors tend to discuss and reflect at great lengths, only, in the end, to deliver their ordinary human words.

La familia rodea al enfermo agrupándose ante sus sienes regresivas, indefensas, sudorosas. Ya no existe hogar sino en torno al velador del pariente enfermo, donde montan guardia impaciente, sus zapatos vacantes, sus cruces de repuesto, sus pildoras de opio. La familia rodea la mesita por espacio de un alto dividendo. Una mujer acomoda en el borde de la mesa, la taza, que casi se ha caído.

Ignoro lo que será del enfermo esta mujer, que le besa y no puede sanarle con el beso, le mira y no puede sanarle con los ojos, le habla y no puede sanarle con el verbo. ¿Es su madre? ¿Y cómo, pues, no puede sanarle? ¿Es su amada? ¿Y cómo, pues, no puede sanarle? ¿Es su hermana? ¿Y cómo, pues, no puede sanarle? ¿Es, simplemente una mujer? ¿Y cómo, pues, no puede sanarle? Porque esta mujer le ha besado, le ha mirado, le ha hablado y hasta le ha cubierto mejor el cuello al enfermo y ¡cosa verdaderamente asombrosa! no le ha sanado.

El paciente contempla su calzado vacante. Traen queso. Llevan tierra. La muerte se acuesta al pie del lecho, a dormir en sus tranquilas aguas y se duerme. Entonces, los libres pies del hombre enfermo, sin menudencias ni pormenores innecesarios, se estiran en acento circunflejo, y se alejan, en una extensión de dos cuerpos de novios, del corazón.

El cirujano ausculta a los enfermos, horas enteras. Hasta donde sus manos cesan de trabajar y empiezan a jugar, las lleva a tientas, rozando la piel de los pacientes, en tanto sus párpados científicos vibran, tocados por la indocta, por la humana flaqueza del amor. Y he visto a esos enfermos morir precisamente del amor desdoblado del cirujano, de los largos diagnósticos, de las dosis exactas, del riguroso análisis de orinas y excrementos. Se rodeaba de improviso un lecho con un biombo. Médicos y enfermeros cruzaban delante del ausente, pizarra triste y próxima, que un niño llenara de números, en un gran monismo de pálidos miles. Cruzaban así, mirando a los otros, como si más irreparable fuese morir de apendicitis o neumonía, y no morir al sesgo del paso de los hombres.

The family surrounds the sick man, gathering before his re-gressive, defenseless, sweating temples. There is no home now other than around the night table of their sick relative, where his empty shoes, his spare crosses, his opium pills impatiently stand guard. The family surrounds the little table for the space of a high dividend. A woman moves a cup, which has almost fallen, on the edge of the table.

I don't know who she is to the sick man, this woman who kisses him and cannot heal him with her kiss, who looks at him and cannot heal him with her eyes, who speaks to him and can-not heal him with her words. Is she his mother? And why, then, can't she heal him? Is she his lover? And why, then, can't she heal him? Is she his sister? And why, then, can't she heal him? Is she just a woman? And why, then, can't she heal him? Be-cause this woman has kissed him, looked at him, spoken to him, and has even better covered the sick man's neck and, a truly amazing thing! has not healed him.

The patient contemplates his empty shoes. They bring cheese. They track in dirt. Death lies down at the foot of the bed, to sleep in its calm waters, and falls asleep. Then the liberated feet of the sick man, with no unnecessary meticulousness or detail, stretch out with a circumflex accent, and increase the distance, by the length of two sweethearts' bodies, from his heart.

The surgeon auscultates the sick, for hours on end. Until his hands quit working and begin to play, he moves them tentatively, brushing against his patients' skins, as his scientific eyelids flutter, moved by the unlettered, by the human weakness of love. And I have seen the sick die precisely from the surgeon's unfolding his love, from his long diagnoses, from his precise dosages, from his rigorous analysis of urine and stool. Suddenly a screen was placed around a bed. Doctors and nurses crossed before the ab-sent one, a sad, at hand blackboard, which a child would fill with numbers, in a great monism of pallid thousands. Yes, so they crossed, looking at the others, as if it were more irreparable to die of appendicitis or pneumonia than aslant the path of men.

Sirviendo a la causa de la religión, vuela con éxito esta mosca, a lo largo de la sala. A la hora de la visita de los cirujanos, sus zumbidos no perdonan el pecho, ciertamente, pero desarrollándose luego, se adueñan del aire, para saludar con genio de mudanza, a los que van a morir. Unos enfermos oyen a esa mosca hasta durante el dolor y de ellos depende, por eso, el linaje del disparo, en las noches tremebundas.

¿Cuánto tiempo ha durado la anestesia, que llaman los hombres? ¡Ciencia de Dios, Teodicea! ¡si se me echa a vivir en tales condiciones, anestesiado totalmente, volteada mi sensibilidad para adentro! ¡Ah doctores de las sales, hombres de las esencias, prójimos de las bases! ¡Pido se me deje con mi tumor de conciencia, con mi irritada lepra sensitiva, ocurra lo que ocurra, aunque me muera! Dejadme dolerme, si lo queréis, mas dejadme despierto de sueño, con todo el universo metido, aunque fuese a las malas, en mi temperatura polvorosa.

En el mundo de la salud perfecta, se reirá por esta perspectiva en que padezco; pero, en el mismo plano y cortando la baraja del juego, percute aquí otra risa de contrapunto.

En la casa del dolor, la queja asalta síncopes de gran compositor, golletes de carácter, que nos hacen cosquillas de verdad, atroces, arduas, y, cumpliendo lo prometido, nos hielan de espantosa incertidumbre.

En la casa del dolor, la queja arranca frontera excesiva. No se reconoce en esta queja de dolor, a la propia queja de la dicha en éxtasis, cuando el amor y la carne se eximen de azor y cuando, al regresar, hay discordia bastante para el diálogo.

¿Dónde está, pues, el otro flanco de esta queja de dolor, si, a estimarla en conjunto, parte ahora del lecho de un hombre?

De la casa del dolor parten quejas tan sordas e inefables y tan colmadas de tanta plenitud que llorar por ellas sería poco, y sería ya mucho sonreír.

Serving the cause of religion, this fly is buzzing with success, the length of the room. At the hour of the surgeons' visit, its buzzings do not excuse the chest, certainly, but then as they develop, they take charge of the air, in order to greet with a character of change, those who are going to die. Some of the sick hear that fly even through their pain and on them, therefore, depends the lineage of the gun shot in the dreadful nights.

How long has anesthesia, which men call it, lasted? Science of God, Theodicea! if I set out to live under such conditions, totally anaesthetized, my sensibility turned upside down! Ah, doctors of salts, men of essences, fellows in doctrine! I ask that you leave me my tumor of consciousness, my irritated, sensitive leprosy, no matter what, even if I die! Let me feel pain, if you so wish, but leave me awake from sleep, with the entire universe involved, though it be for the worse, in my dusty fever.

In the world of perfect health, this perspective I suffer in will be a source of laughter; but, on the same plane, and cutting the deck for the game, another laugh ricochets here in counterpoint.

In the house of pain, the moan assaults the syncopes of a great composer, gullets of character, that produce true, savage, arduous tickling, and, fulfilling what is promised, chill us with frightening uncertainty.

In the house of pain, the moan tears away superfluous frontage. Not recognized in this moan of pain is the very moan of happiness in ecstasy, when love and flesh exempt each other from confusion and when, on return, there is sufficient discord for dialogue.

Where then, is the other side of this moan of pain, if to value it as a whole, it now issues from a man's bed?

From the house of sorrow issue moans so muffled and ineffable and so overflowing with plentitude that to weep for them would be little, and to smile would be a lot.

Se atumulta la sangre en el termómetro.

¡No es grato morir, señor, si en la vida nada se deja y si en la
muerte nada es posible, sino sobre lo que se deja en la vida!
¡No es grato morir, señor, si en la vida nada se deja y si en la
muerte nada es posible, sino sobre lo que se deja en la vida!
¡No es grato morir, señor, si en la vida nada se deja y si en la
muerte nada es posible, sino lo que pudo dejarse en la vida!

—1924

Blood storms in the thermometer.

It is not pleasant to die, Señor, if in life nothing is left and if in
death nothing is possible, if not what one leaves in life!
It is not pleasant to die, Señor, if in life nothing is left and if in
death nothing is possible, if not what one leaves in life!
It is not pleasant to die, Señor, if in life nothing is left and if in
death nothing is possible, if not what could be left in life!

—*1924*

El momento más grave de la vida

Un hombre dijo:

—El momento más grave de mi vida estuvo en la batalla del Marne, cuando fui herido en el pecho.

Otro hombre dijo:

—El momento más grave de mi vida, ocurrió en un maremoto de Yokohama, del cual salvé milagrosamente, refugiado bajo el alero de una tienda de lacas.

Y otro hombre dijo:

—El momento más grave de mi vida acontece cuando duermo de día.

Y otro dijo:

—El momento más grave de mi vida ha estado en mi mayor soledad.

Y otro dijo:

—El momento más grave de mi vida fue mi prisión en una cárcel del Perú.

Y otro dijo:

The Lowest Moment of My Life

A man said:

"The lowest moment of my life came during the battle of the Marne, when I was wounded in the chest."

Another man said:

"The lowest moment of my life occurred during a tidal wave in Yokohama, from which I was miraculously saved when I took cover beneath the overhang of a lacquer shop."

And another man said:

"The lowest moment of my life comes when I sleep during the day."

And another said:

"The lowest moment of my life has been during my most profound loneliness."

And another said:

"The lowest moment of my life was when I was in jail in Peru."

And another said:

—El momento más grave de mi vida es el haber sorprendido de perfil a mi padre.

Y el último hombre dijo:

—El momento más grave de mi vida no ha llegado todavía.

"The lowest moment of my life is having unexpectedly seen my father in profile."

And the last man said:

"The lowest moment of my life hasn't happened yet."

Nómina de huesos

Se pedía a grandes voces:
—Que muestre las dos manos a la vez.
Y esto no fue posible.
—Que, mientras llora, le tomen la medida de sus pasos.
Y esto no fue posible.
—Que piense un pensamiento idéntico, en el tiempo en que
un cero permanece inútil.
Y esto no fue posible.
—Que haga una locura.
Y esto no fue posible.
—Que entre él y otro hombre semejante a él, se interponga
una muchedumbre de hombres como él.
Y esto no fue posible.
—Que le comparen consigo mismo.
Y esto no fue posible.
—Que le llamen, en fin, por su nombre.
Y esto no fue posible.

—*1924/1925*

Bone Nomenclature

They asked at the top of their lungs:
"Have him show both hands at once."
And this was not possible.
"As he's crying, let them take the measure of his footsteps."
And this was not possible.
"Have him think an identical thought in the length of time a zero remains useless."
And this was not possible.
"Have him do something crazy."
And this was not possible.
"Have a crowd of men like him post themselves between him and another man like him."
And this was not possible.
"Have them compare him with himself."
And this was not possible.
"Have them, at last, call him by his name."
And this was not possible.

—*1924/1925*

Voy a hablar de la esperanza

Yo no sufro este dolor como César Vallejo. Yo no me duelo ahora como artista, como hombre ni como simple ser vivo siquiera. Yo no sufro este dolor como católico, como mahometano ni como ateo. Hoy sufro solamente. Si no me llamase César Vallejo, también sufriría este mismo dolor. Si no fuese artista, también lo sufriría. Si no fuese hombre ni ser vivo siquiera, también lo sufriría. Si no fuese católico, ateo ni mahometano, también lo sufriría. Hoy sufro desde más a bajo. Hoy sufro solamente.

Me duelo ahora sin explicaciones. Mi dolor es tan hondo, que no tuvo ya causa ni carece de causa. ¿Qué sería su causa? ¿Dónde está aquello tan importante, que dejase de ser su causa? Nada es su causa; nada ha podido dejar de ser su causa. ¿A qué ha nacido este dolor, por sí mismo? Mi dolor es del viento del norte y del viento del sur, como esos huevos neutros que algunas aves raras ponen del viento. Si hubiera muerto mi novia, mi dolor sería igual. Si me hubieran cortado el cuello de raíz, mi dolor sería igual. Si la vida fuese, en fin, de otro modo, mi dolor sería igual. Hoy sufro desde más arriba. Hoy sufro solamente.

Miro el dolor del hambriento y veo que su hambre anda tan lejos de mi sufrimiento, que de quedarme ayuno hasta morir, saldría siempre de mi tumba una brizna de yerba al menos. Lo mismo el enamorado. ¡Qué sangre la suya más engendrada, para la mía sin fuente ni consumo!

Yo creía basta ahora que todas las cosas del universo eran, inevitablemente, padres o hijos. Pero he aquí que mi dolor de

I Am Going to Talk About Hope

I do not suffer this pain as César Vallejo. I don't hurt now as an artist, as a man, or even a simple living being. I don't suffer this pain as a Catholic, a Muslim, or an atheist. Today I simply suffer. If I weren't named César Vallejo, I would suffer the same pain. If I weren't an artist, I would still suffer. If I weren't a man or even a living being, yes, I would suffer it. If I weren't a Catholic, an atheist, or a Muslim, I would suffer just the same. Today I suffer from a place farther down. Today I simply suffer.

I suffer now without explanation. My pain is so deep that there was never a cause or a lack of cause. What would the cause be? Where is there something so important that it would cease to be the cause? Nothing is the cause; nothing has been able to cease being the cause. Why was this pain born? For itself? My pain comes on the wind of the north and the wind of the south, like those neuter eggs some rare birds lay on the wind. If my sweetheart had died, my pain would be the same. If life were, in sum, different, my pain would be the same. Today I suffer farther up. Today I simply suffer.

I observe the pain of a hungry man and I see that hunger is so far from my suffering that even if I fasted till I died, a sprig of wheat would still sprout from my tomb. The same for the lover. How rich with begetting his blood compared to mine with no flowing spring or utilization.

I thought till now that all things of the universe were, inevitably, fathers or sons. But today I see that my pain is not that of either a father or a son. It is as lacking in spine at nightfall as

hoy no es padre ni es hijo. Le falta espalda para anochecer, tanto como le sobra pecho para amanecer y si lo pusiesen en una estancia obscura, no daría luz y si lo pusiesen en una estancia luminosa, no echaría sombra. Hoy sufro suceda lo que suceda. Hoy sufro solamente.

it is supplied with courage at dawn, and if it were put in a dark room, it would not give light and if put in a bright room, it would not cast a shadow. Today I suffer no matter what happens. Today I simply suffer.

Altura y pelos

¿Quién no tiene su vestido azul?
¿Quién no almuerza y no toma el tranvía,
con su cigarrillo contratado y su dolor de bolsillo?
¡Yo que tan sólo he nacido!
¡Yo que tan sólo he nacido!

¿Quién no escribe una carta?
¿Quién no habla de un asunto muy importante,
muriendo de costumbre y llorando de oído?
¡Yo que solamente he nacido!
¡Yo que solamente he nacido!

¿Quién no se llama Carlos o cualquier otra cosa?
¿Quién al gato no dice gato gato?
¡Ay, yo que sólo he nacido solamente!
¡Ay, yo que sólo he nacido solamente!

—1927

Height and Hair

Who doesn't have his blue suit?
Who doesn't eat lunch or take the trolley
with his hired cigarette and pain in his pocket?
I who only have been born!
I who only have been born!

Who doesn't write a letter?
Who doesn't talk about a very important matter,
dying from habit and weeping from hearing?
I who only have been born!
I who only have been born!

Who isn't named Carlos or anything else?
Who doesn't say kitty kitty to the cat?
Ay! I who only, solely, have been born!
Ay! I who only, solely, have been born!

—1927

Hasta el día en que vuelva, de esta piedra
nacerá mi talón definitivo,
con su juego de crímenes, su yedra,
su obstinación dramática, su olivo.

Hasta el día en que vuelva, prosiguiendo,
con franca rectitud de cojo amargo,
de pozo en pozo, mi periplo, entiendo
que el hombre ha de ser bueno, sin embargo.

Hasta el día en que vuelva y hasta que ande
el animal que soy, entre sus jueces,
nuestro bravo meñique será grande,
digno, infinito dedo entre los dedos.

Until the Day I Come Back,
from This Rock . . .

Until the day I come back, from this rock
will be born my definitive heel,
with its set of crimes, its ivy,
its dramatic obstinacy, its olive tree.

Until the day I come back, continuing,
with the candid rectitude of a bitter lame man,
from well to well, my odyssey, I understand
that man must, nonetheless, be good.

Until the day I come back and until
the animal I am walks among his judges,
our brave little finger will be big,
worthy, an infinite finger among fingers.

Hoy me gusta la vida mucho menos,
pero siempre me gusta vivir: yo lo decía.
Casi toqué la parte de mi todo y me contuve
con un tiro en la lengua detrás de mi palabra.

Hoy me palpo el mentón en retirada
y en estos momentáneos pantalones yo me digo:
¡Tánta vida y jamás!
¡Tántos años y siempre mis semanas! . . .
Mis padres enterrados con su piedra
y su triste estirón que no ha acabado;
de cuerpo entero hermanos, mis hermanos,
y, en fin, mi sér parado y en chaleco.

Me gusta la vida enormemente,
pero, desde luego,
con mi muerte querida y mi café
y viendo los castaños frondosos de París
y diciendo:
Es un ojo éste, aquél; una frente ésta, aquélla . . .
Y repitiendo:
¡Tánta vida y jamás me falla la tonada!
¡Tántos años y siempre, siempre, siempre!

Dije chaleco, dije
todo, parte, ansia, dije casi, por no llorar.
Que es verdad que sufrí en aquel hospital que queda al lado

Today I Am Much Less Fond
of Life . . .

Today I am much less fond of life,
but I always like living; I've said that before.
I almost touched part of my whole but stopped myself
with a shot to the tongue behind my word.

Today I stroke my chin in retreat
and in these momentary trousers say to myself:
So much life and never!
So many years and always my weeks!
My parents buried beneath their stone
and their sad strong pull that hasn't ended;
brothers whole in body, my brothers,
and, finally, my self, idle, and in a vest.

I like life enormously
but, of course,
with my beloved death and my café
and seeing the luxuriant chestnut trees of Paris
and saying:
This is one eye, that: this a forehead, and that . . .
    And repeating:
so much life and the tune never lets me down!
So many years and always, always, always!

I said vest, I said
all, part, yearning, I said almost, to keep from crying.
For it is true that I suffered in that hospital nearby

y está bien y está mal haber mirado
de abajo para arriba mi organismo.

Me gustará vivir siempre, así fuese de barriga,
porque, como iba diciendo y lo repito,
¡tánta vida y jamás! ¡Y tántos años,
y siempre, mucho siempre, siempre siempre!

—*1931/1932*

and it's good and it's bad to have looked over
my organism from bottom to top.

I would like to live forever, even if on my belly,
because, as I was saying and I repeat,
so much life and never! And so many years,
and always, much always, always always!

—*1931/1932*

Epístola a los transeúntes

Reanudo mi día de conejo,
mi noche de elefante en descanso.

Y, entre mi, digo:
ésta es mi inmensidad en bruto, a cántaros,
éste mi grato peso, que me buscara abajo para pájaro;
éste es mi brazo
que por su cuenta rehusó ser ala,
éstas son mis sagradas escrituras,
éstos mis alarmados compañones.

Lúgubre isla me alumbrará continental,
mientras el capitolio se apoye en mi íntimo derrumbe
y la asamblea en lanzas clausure mi desfile.

Pero cuando yo muera
de vida y no de tiempo,
cuando lleguen a dos mis dos maletas,
éste ha de ser mi estómago en que cupo mi lámpara en
    pedazos,
ésta aquella cabeza que expió los tormentos del círculo
    en mis pasos,
éstos esos gusanos que el corazón contó por unidades,
éste ha de ser mi cuerpo solidario
por el que vela el alma individual; éste ha de ser
mi hombligo en que maté mis piojos natos,
ésta mi cosa cosa, mi cosa tremebunda.

Epistle to Passersby

I begin anew my day of a rabbit,
my night of an elephant at rest.

And, to myself I say:
this is my raw immensity, by the brimming pitcherful,
this is my welcome weight, look farther down for a songbird;
this is my arm
that on its own refused to be a wing,
these are my sacred writings,
these my alarmed cuillons.

Lugubrious island will light me continentally,
while the Capitolio rests on my intimate collapse
and an up-in-arms assembly brings my parade to a close.

But when I die
of life and not of time,
when my two suitcases reach the count of two,
this will have to be my stomach that held the broken pieces
    of my lamp,
this the head that atoned for the torments of the circle in my
    steps,
these those worms my heart counted by the units,
this will have to be my solidarity body
over which the individual soul keeps watch; this has to be
my humbilicus in which I killed my innate lice,
this is my thing thing, my fear-instilling thing.

En tanto, convulsiva, ásperamente
convalece mi freno,
sufriendo como sufro del lenguaje directo del león;
y, puesto que he existido entre dos potestades de ladrillo,
convalezco yo mismo, sonriendo de mis labios.

—1932

   Meanwhile, convulsively, harshly,
my restraint convalesces,
suffering as I suffer from the direct language of the lion;
and, given that I have lived between two potentates of brick,
I myself am convalescing, smiling from my lips.

                       —1932

Confianza en el anteojo, no en el ojo;
en la escalera, nunca en el peldaño;
en el ala, nó en el ave
y en ti sólo, en ti sólo, en ti sólo.

Confianza en la maldad, no en el malvado;
en el vaso, mas nunca en el licor;
en el cadáver, no en el hombre
y en ti sólo, en ti sólo, en ti sólo.

Confianza en muchos, pero ya no en uno;
en el cauce, jamás en la corriente;
en los calzones, no en las piernas
y en ti sólo, en ti sólo, en ti sólo.

Confianza en la ventana, no en la puerta;
en la madre, mas no en los nueve meses;
en el destino, no en el dado de oro,
y en ti sólo, en ti sólo, en ti sólo.

—5 *Octubre 1937*

Reliance on the Eyeglasses,
Not the Eye . . .

Reliance on the eyeglasses, not the eye;
on the stairway, never the step;
on the wing, not the bird
and on you only, you only, you only.

Reliance on evil, not the evildoer;
on the glass, but never the liquor;
on the corpse, not the man
and on you only, you only, you only.

Reliance on many, and no longer on one;
on the channel, never the current;
on the trousers, not the legs
and on you only, you only, you only.

Reliance on the window, not the door;
on the mother, but not the nine months;
on destiny, not the gold die,
and on you only, you only, you only.

—October 5, 1937

Quisiera hoy ser feliz de buena gana,
ser feliz y portarme frondoso de preguntas,
abrir por temperamento de par en par mi cuarto,
    como loco,
y reclamar, en fin,
en mi confianza física acostado,
sólo por ver si quieren,
sólo por ver si quieren probar de mi espontánea
    posición,
reclamar, voy diciendo,
por qué me dan así tánto en el alma.

Pues quisiera en sustancia ser dichoso,
obrar sin bastón, laica humildad, ni
    burro negro.
Así las sensaciones de este mundo,
los cantos subjuntivos,
el lápiz que perdí en mi cavidad
y mis amados órganos de llanto.

Hermano persuasible, camarada,
padre por la grandeza, hijo mortal,
amigo y contendor, inmenso documento de
    Darwin:
¿a qué hora, pues, vendrán con mi retrato?
¿A los goces? ¿Acaso sobre goce amortajado?
¿Más temprano? ¿Quién sabe, a las porfías?

Today I Would Like to Be Happy Willingly . . .

Today I would like to be happy willingly,
to be happy and go about leafy with questions,
because of my nature, to throw wide open my room,
   like a madman,
and to protest, in short,
settled in my physical trust
only to see if they want,
only to see if they want to test my spontaneous
   position,
to protest, I am saying,
why they are hitting me so hard in my soul.

Well, in a word, I would like to be happy,
to proceed without a cane, secular humility, or
   black burro.
So are the sensations of this world,
the subjunctive songs,
the pencil I lost in my cavity
and my beloved organs for weeping.

Persuadable brother, comrade,
father for greatness, mortal son,
friend and antagonist, extraordinary document of
   Darwin:
at what hour, then, will they come with my portrait?
At their pleasure? Perhaps pleasure shrouded?
Sooner than that? Who knows, importuned?

A las misericordias, camarada,
hombre mío en rechazo y observación, vecino
en cuyo cuello enorme sube y baja,
al natural; sin hilo, mi esperanza . . .

—*1937*

Prayers for mercy, comrade,
my fellow in rejection and observation, neighbor
on whose enormous neck rises and falls,
spontaneously, without a string, my hope.

—*1937*

¡Y si después de tantas palabras,
no sobrevive la palabra!
¡Si después de las alas de los pájaros,
no sobrevive el pájaro parado!
¡Más valdría, en verdad,
que se lo coman todo y acabemos!

¡Haber nacido para vivir de nuestra muerte!
¡Levantarse del cielo hacia la tierra
por sus propios desastres
y espiar el momento de apagar con su sombra su
    tiniebla!
¡Más valdría, francamente,
que se lo coman todo y qué más da! . . .

¡Y si después de tánta historia, sucumbimos,
no ya de eternidad,
sino de esas cosas sencillas, como estar
en la casa o ponerse a cavilar!
¡Y si luego encontramos,
de buenas a primeras, que vivimos,
a juzgar por la altura de los astros,
por el peine y las manchas del pañuelo!
¡Más valdría, en verdad,
que se lo coman todo, desde luego!

Se dirá que tenemos
en uno de los ojos mucha pena

And If After So Many Words . . .

And if after so many words,
the word does not survive!
If after the wings of the birds,
the bird on the ground does not survive!
Much better, truthfully,
for it all to fizzle and get it over with!

To have been born to live off our deaths!
To rise from heaven toward the Earth
by way of our own disasters
and glimpse the moment to extinguish our darkness with
    our shadow!
Much better, frankly,
for it all to fizzle and who cares!

And if after so much history, we succumb,
now not from eternity,
but from those simple things, like being
at home, or starting to think things over!
And if we then find,
unexpectedly, that we are living,
to judge by the height of the stars,
by the comb and the handkerchief stains!
Much better, truthfully,
for it all to fizzle, of course!

It will be said that we have
a lot of sadness in one eye

y también en el otro, mucha pena
y en los dos, cuando miran, mucha pena. . . .
Entonces . . . ¡Claro! . . . Entonces . . . ¡ni palabra!

—*1936*

and also in the other, a lot of sadness
and in both, when they are looking, a lot of sadness. . . .
Then . . . Of course! Then . . . Not a word!

—*1936*

Los nueve monstruos

I, desgraciadamente,
el dolor crece en el mundo a cada rato,
crece a treinta minutos por segundo, paso a paso,
y la naturaleza del dolor, es el dolor dos veces
y la condición del martirio, carnívora, voraz,
es el dolor dos veces
y la función de la yerba purísima, el dolor
dos veces
y el bien de sér, dolernos doblemente.

Jamás, hombres humanos,
hubo tánto dolor en el pecho, en la solapa, en la cartera,
en el vaso, en la carnicería, en la aritmética!
Jamás tánto cariño doloroso,
jamás tan cerca arremetió lo lejos,
jamás el fuego nunca
jugó mejor su rol de frío muerto!
Jamás, señor ministro de salud, fue la salud
más mortal
y la migraña extrajo tánta frente de la frente!
Y el mueble tuvo en su cajón, dolor,
el corazón, en su cajón, dolor,
la lagartija, en su cajón, dolor.

Crece la desdicha, hermanos hombres,
más pronto que la máquina, a diez máquinas, y crece
con la res de Rousseau, con nuestras barbas;
crece el mal por razones que ignoramos

Nine Monsters

So, unfortunately,
sorrow grows in the world at every instant,
grows at thirty minutes per second, little by little,
and the nature of sorrow, is sorrow twice over,
and the carnivorous, voracious state of martyrdom
is sorrow twice over
and the function of the purest *maté*, sorrow
twice over,
and the well-being of self, to pain us doubly.

Never, fellow men,
was there such sorrow in our chest, lapel, billfold,
glass, the butcher shop, arithmetic!
Never so much sorrowful affection,
never did distance attack so near,
never did fire ever
play the role of a cold corpse better!
Never, Señor Minister of Health, was health
more subject to death
nor did the migraine extract so much forehead from the forehead!
And the cupboard had, in its drawer, sorrow,
the heart, in its drawer, sorrow,
the lizard, in its drawer, sorrow.

Misfortune grows, brother men,
more quickly than the machine, than ten machines, and it grows
with Rousseau's beast, with our whiskers;
evil grows for reasons we do not know

y es una inundación con propios líquidos,
con propio barro y propia nube sólida!
Invierte el sufrimiento posiciones, da función
en que el humor acuoso es vertical
al pavimento,
el ojo es visto y esta oreja oída,
y esta oreja da nueve campanadas a la hora
del rayo, y nueve carcajadas
a la hora del trigo, y nueve sones hembras
a la hora del llanto, y nueve cánticos
a la hora del hambre y nueve truenos
y nueve látigos, menos un grito.

El dolor nos agarra, hermanos hombres,
por detrás, de perfil,
y nos aloca en los cinemas,
nos clava en los gramófonos,
nos desclava en los lechos, cae perpendicularmente
a nuestros boletos, a nuestras cartas;
y es muy grave sufrir, puede uno orar . . .
Pues de resultas
del dolor, hay algunos
que nacen, otros crecen, otros mueren,
y otros que nacen y no mueren, otros
que sin haber nacido, mueren, y otros
que no nacen ni mueren (son los más)

Y también de resultas
del sufrimiento, estoy triste
hasta la cabeza, y más triste hasta el tobillo,
de ver al pan, crucificado, al nabo,
ensagrentado,
llorando, a la cebolla,
al cereal, en general, harina,
a la sal, hecha polvo, al agua, huyendo,
al vino, un ecce-homo,
tan pálida a la nieve, al sol tan ardio!
¡Cómo, hermanos humanos;

and it is an inundation with its own liquids,
with its own mud and its own solid cloud!
Suffering inverts positions, performs a function
in which aqueous humor is vertical
to the pavement,
the eye is seeing and this ear hearing,
and this ear strikes nine o'clock on the hour
of the lightning flash, and nine belly laughs
at the hour of wheat, and nine female sounds
at the hour of weeping, and nine canticles
at the hour of hunger and nine thunderclaps
and nine whips, minus a scream.

Sorrow seizes us, brother men,
from behind, from the side,
and maddens us in the cinema,
it nails us in gramophones,
unnails us in beds, falls perpendicularly
to our tickets, to our letters;
and it is very grave to suffer, one can pray . . .
For of the results
of sorrow, there are some
who are born, others grow, others die,
and others are born and don't die, others
that without having been born, die, and others
that neither are born nor die (they're the majority)

And also of the results
of suffering, I am sad
up to my head, and sadder down to my ankle,
from seeing bread, crucified, the turnip,
all bloody,
the onion, weeping,
grain, usually, flour,
salt, ground to powder, water fleeing,
wine, an *Ecce Homo,*
the snow so pale, the sun so ardeity!
How, brother humans,

no deciros que ya no puedo y
ya no puedo con tánto cajón,
tánto minuto, tánta
lagartija y tánta
inversión, tánto lejos y tánta sed de sed!
Señor Ministro de Salud: ¿qué hacer?
¡Ah! desgraciadamente, hombres humanos,
hay, hermanos, muchísimo que hacer

—*3 Noviembre 1937*

not tell you that I can do no more and
now I cannot cope with so much drawer,
so much minute, so much
lizard and so much
inversion, so much distance and so much thirst of thirst!
Señor Minister of Health, what to do?
Ah! unfortunately, fellow men,
there is, brothers, much to be done.

—*November 3, 1937*

Me viene, hay días, una gana ubérrima, política,
de querer, de besar al cariño en sus dos rostros,
y me viene de lejos un querer
demostrativo, otro querer amar, de grado o fuerza,
al que me odia, al que rasga su papel, al muchachito,
a la que llora por el que lloraba,
al rey del vino, al esclavo del agua,
al que ocultóse en su ira,
al que suda, al que pasa, al que sacude su persona en
    mi alma.
Y quiero, por lo tanto, acomodarle
al que me habla, su trenza; sus cabellos, al soldado;
su luz, al grande; su grandeza, al chico.
Quiero planchar directamente
un pañuelo al que no puede llorar
y, cuando estoy triste o me duele la dicha,
remendar a los niños y a los genios.

    Quiero ayudar al bueno a ser su poquillo de malo
y me urge estar sentado
a la diestra del zurdo, y responder al mudo,
tratando de serle útil en
lo que puedo, y también quiero muchísimo
lavarle al cojo el pie,
y ayudarle a dormir al tuerto próximo.

    ¡Ah querer, éste, el mío, éste, el mundial,
interhumano y parroquial, provecto!

There Are Days I Am Struck by an Overflowing, Politic Longing . . .

There are days I am struck by an overflowing, politic longing
to love, to kiss affection on its two faces,
and from afar I am struck by a demonstrative
longing, another wanting to love, willingly or by force,
the one who loathes me, the one who rips his paper, the boy,
the woman who weeps for the man who wept,
the king of wine, the slave of water,
the one who hid in his anger.
the one who sweats, the one who goes by, the one who shakes
    his person in my soul.
And I want, therefore, to adjust his braid
for the one who talks to me; for the soldier, his hair;
for the great one, his illumination; for the boy, his greatness.
I want personally to iron
a handkerchief for the one who cannot cry
and, when I am sad or my happiness pains me,
to patch together children and geniuses.

I want to help the good man to be his modicum of bad
and it is urgent for me to be seated
at the right hand of the left-handed, and to reply to the mute one,
trying to be useful to him in
all that I can, and also I want very much
to wash the foot of the lame man,
and to help the one-eyed man near me sleep.

Ah to love, this one, mine, this one, the world's
interhuman and parochial, well advanced in years!

Me viene a pelo,
desde el cimiento, desde la ingle pública,
y, viniendo de lejos, da ganas de besarle
la bufanda al cantor,
y al que sufre, besarle en su sartén,
al sordo, en su rumor craneano, impávido;
al que me da lo que olvidé en mi seno,
en su Dante, en su Chaplin, en sus hombros.

   Quiero, para terminar,
cuando estoy al borde célebre de la violencia
o lleno de pecho el corazón, querría
ayudar a reír al que sonríe,
ponerle un pajarillo al malvado en plena nuca,
cuidar a los enfermos enfadándolos,
comprarle al vendedor,
ayudarle a matar al matador—cosa terrible—
y quisiera yo ser bueno conmigo
en todo.

                              —6 *Noviembre 1937*

It strikes me, opportunely,
from the foundation, from the public groin,
and, coming from afar, makes me long to kiss
the cantor's scarf,
and to kiss the one who suffers on his fry pan,
the deaf man, on his dauntless, cranial murmur;
the one who gives me what I forgot in my bosom,
on his Dante, on his Chaplin, on his shoulders.

    I want, in order to bring this to a close,
when I am on the famous edge of violence
or my heart is filled with courage, I would like
to help the one who smiles laugh,
to set a little bird right on the nape of the villain's neck,
to irritate the ill by looking after them,
to buy from the seller,
to help the killer kill—terrible thing—
and I would like to be good to myself
in all things.

—November 6, 1937

Piedra negra sobre una piedra blanca

Me moriré en París con aguacero,
un día del cual tengo ya el recuerdo.
Me moriré en París—y no me corro—
talvez un jueves, como es hoy, de otoño.

Jueves será, porque hoy, jueves, que proso
estos versos, los húmeros me he puesto
a la mala y, jamás como hoy, me he vuelto,
con todo mi camino, a verme solo.

César Vallejo ha muerto, le pegaban
todos sin que él les haga nada;
le daban duro con un palo y duro

también con una soga; son testigos
los días jueves y los huesos húmeros,
la soledad, la lluvia, los caminos . . .

Black Stone on a White Stone

I shall die in Paris when it's pouring rain,
a day that I already remember.
I shall die in Paris—and I don't go far—
maybe a Thursday, like today, in autumn.

It will be Thursday, because today, Thursday, as I am
prosing these lines, my humeri have brought me to my knees
and never, as I did today, have I turned,
with all my road before me, and seen myself alone.

César Vallejo has died, they all beat him
though he did nothing to them;
they laid it on hard with a stick and hard

also with a rope; witnesses to it are
the Thursdays and the humeri,
the loneliness, the rain, the roads . . .

Poema para ser leído y cantado

Sé que hay una persona
que me busca en su mano, día y noche,
encontrándome, a cada minuto, en su calzado.
¿Ignora que la noche está enterrada
con espuelas detrás de la cocina?

Sé que hay una persona compuesta de mis partes,
a la que integro cuando va mi talle
cabalgando en su exacta piedrecilla.
¿Ignora que a su cofre
no volverá moneda que salió con su retrato?

Sé el día,
pero el sol se me ha escapado;
sé el acto universal que hizo en su cama
con ajeno valor y esa agua tibia, cuya
superficial frecuencia es una mina.
¿Tan pequeña es, acaso, esa persona,
que hasta sus propios pies así la pisan?

Un gato es el lindero entre ella y yo,
al lado mismo de su tasa de agua.
La veo en las esquinas, se abre y cierra
su veste, antes palmera interrogante . . .
¿Qué podrá hacer sino cambiar de llanto?

Pero me busca y busca. ¡Es una historia!

—7 Septiembre 1937

Poem to Be Read and Sung

I know there is a person
who looks for me in his hand, day and night,
finding me, at every minute, in his shoes and socks.
Doesn't he know that night is buried
with spurs behind the kitchen?

I know there is a person composed of my parts,
whom I unify when my waist goes by
on horseback on its precise little stone.
Doesn't he know that no coin
will come back to his coffer that left with his image?

I know the day,
but the sun has escaped me;
I know the universal act he performed on his bed
with the courage of another and that lukewarm water, whose
superficial frequency is a mine.
So small, then, is that person
that even his own feet step on him like that?

A cat is the boundary between that person and me,
at the very edge of its measure of water.
I see that person on street corners, opening and closing
his garments, previously a questioning palm tree . . .
What can he do but change his weeping?

But he looks and looks for me. That's a story for you.

—*September 7, 1937*

La vida, esta vida
me placía, su instrumento, esas palomas . . .
Me placía escucharlas gobernarse en lontananza,
advenir naturales, determinado el número,
y ejecutar, según sus aflicciones, sus dianas de animales.

Encogido,
oí desde mis hombros
su sosegada producción,
cave los albañales sesgar sus trece huesos,
dentro viejo tormillo hincharse el plomo.
Sus paujiles picos,
pareadas palomitas,
las póbridas, hojeándose los hígados,
sobrinas de la nube . . . Vida! Vida! Esta es la vida!

Zurear su tradición rojo les era,
rojo moral, palomas vigilantes, talvez rojo de herrumbre,
si caían entonces azulmente.

Su elemental cadena,
sus viajes de individuales pájaros viajeros,
echaron humo denso,
pena física, pórtico influyente.

Life, This Life . . .

Life, this life
was pleasing, its instrument, those doves . . .
It was pleasing to hear them in the distance, running their
   government,
accustomed arrival, their number determined,
performing, according to their afflictions, their animal reveille.

Hunched,
I heard from my shoulders
their calm proceedings,
dig the cesspools skew their thirteen bones,
inside the old screw expanding lead.
Their cashew bird beaks,
diminutive doves,
pomoldering, livers rustling like leaves,
nieces of the cloud . . . Life! Life! This is life!

Cooing was to them their red tradition,
moral red, vigilant doves,
perhaps red from rust,
if they then fell bluely.

Their elemental chain,
their journeys of individual migrating birds,
emitted dense smoke,
physical pain, influential portico.

Palomas saltando, indelebles
palomas olorosas,
manferidas venían, advenían
por azarosas vías digestivas,
a contarme sus cosas fosforosas,
pájaros de contar,
pájaros transitivos y orejones . . .

No escucharé ya más desde mis hombros
huesudo, enfermo, en cama,
ejecutar sus dianas de animales . . . Me doy cuenta.
—*1936*

Doves hopping, indelible
aromatic doves,
assayed, they came, arrived
via hazardous digestive routes
to tell me their phosphorosy news,
tale-telling birds,
transitive, Incanoble birds . . .
I shall not again hear them from my bony
shoulders, sick in bed,
performing their animal reveilles . . . I realize that.

—*1936*

París, Octubre 1936

De todo esto yo soy el único que parte.
De este banco me voy, de mis calzones,
de mi gran situación, de mis acciones,
de mi número hendido parte a parte,
de todo esto yo soy el único que parte.

De los Campos Elíseos o al dar vuelta
la extraña callejuela de la Luna,
mi defunción se va, parte mi cuna,
y, rodeada de gente, sola, suelta,
mi semejanza humana dase vuelta
y despacha sus sombras una a una.

Y me alejo de todo, porque todo
se queda para hacer la coartada:
mi zapato, su ojal, también su lodo
y hasta el doblez del codo
de mi propia camisa abotonada.

Paris, October 1936

Of all this I am the only one departing.
From this bench I am leaving, from my trousers,
from my grand situation, from my actions,
from my number split wide apart,
of all this I am the only one departing.

From the Champs Elysées or at the turning
of the strange little la Lune alleyway,
my demise is leaving, my cradle departing,
and, surrounded with people, alone, unattached,
my human semblance turns
and dispatches its shadows one by one.

And I move away from it all, because everything
is staying behind to provide the alibi:
my shoe, its eyelet, also its mud
and even the bend at the elbow
of my own buttoned up shirt.

Despedida recordando un adiós

Al cabo, al fin, por último,
torno, volví y acábome y os gimo, dándoos
la llave, mi sombrero, esta cartita para todos.
Al cabo de la llave está el metal en que aprendiéramos
a desdorar el oro, y está, al fin,
de mi sombrero, este pobre cerebro mal peinado,
y, último vaso de humo, en su papel dramático,
yace este sueño práctico del alma.

¡Adiós, hermanos san pedros,
heráclitos, erasmos, espinozas!
¡Adiós, tristes obispos bolcheviques!
¡Adiós, gobernadores en desorden!
¡Adiós, vino que está en al agua como vino!
¡Adiós, alcohol que está en la lluvia!

¡Adiós también, me digo a mí mismo,
adiós, vuelo formal de los milígramos!
¡También adiós, de modo idéntico,
frío del frío y frío del calor!
Al cabo, al fin, por último, la lógica,
los linderos del fuego,
la despedida recordando aquel adiós.

—*12 Octubre 1937*

Farewell Recalling an Adiós

At the end, finally, at last,
I turn, I returned, and I end it and I moan you, handing you
the key, my hat, this brief letter for everyone.
At the end of the key is the metal on which we might have
    learned
to ungild gold, and there, at the end
of my hat, is this poor badly combed brain,
and, last glass of smoke, in its dramatic role,
lies this practical dream of the soul.

¡Adiós, brother Saint Peters,
Heracliti, Erasmi, Spinozas!
¡Adiós, sad Bolshevik bishops!
¡Adiós, governors in disarray!
¡Adiós, wine that's in water like wine!
¡Adiós, alcohol that's in the rain!

¡Adiós to you, too, I tell myself,
adiós, formal flight of the milligrams!
Also adiós, in exactly the same manner,
cold of the cold and cold of the heat!
At the end, finally, at last, logic,
the boundaries of fire,
the farewell recalling that adiós.

—*October 12, 1937*

Y no me digan nada,
que uno puede matar perfectamente,
ya que, sudando tinta,
uno hace cuanto puede, no me digan . . .

Volveremos, señores, a vernos con manzanas;
tarde la criatura pasará,
la expresión de Aristóteles armada
de grandes corazones de madera,
la de Heráclito injerta en la de Marx,
la del suave sonando rudamente . . .
Es lo que bien narraba mi garganta:
uno puede matar perfectamente.

Señores,
caballeros, volveremos a vernos sin paquetes;
hasta entonces exijo, exijiré de mi flaqueza
el acento del día, que,
según veo, estuvo ya esperándome en mi lecho.
Y exijo del sombrero la infausta analogía del recuerdo,
ya que, a veces, asumo con éxito mi inmensidad llorada,
ya que, a veces, me ahogo en la voz de mi vecino
y padezco
contando en maíces los años,
cepillando mi ropa al son de un muerto
o sentado borracho en mi ataúd . . .

—*1931/1932*

And Don't Say a Word to Me . . .

And don't say a word to me,
nothing about how one can kill perfectly,
seeing that, sweating ink,
one does what one can, don't say a . . .

We will see one another again, señores, with apples;
late, the child will pass by,
Aristotle's expression fortified
with great hearts of wood,
Heraclitus's expression grafted onto Marx,
that of the smooth ringing harshly . . .
It is just as my throat narrated so well:
one can kill perfectly.7

Señores,
caballeros, we will see one another again without packages;
until then I make demands, I shall demand of my weakness
the accent of the day, which,
as I see it, was already waiting in my bed.
And from my hat I demand the ruinous analogy of memory,
since, at times, I successfully assume my bewailed immensity,
since, at times, I drown in the voice of my neighbor
and I suffer
counting in kernels the years,
brushing my clothing to the tune of a dead man
or sitting drunk in my coffin . . .

—1931/1932

En suma, no poseo para expresar mi vida, sino mi muerte.

Y, después de todo, al cabo de la escalonada naturaleza y del gorrión en bloque, me duermo, mano a mano con mi sombra.

Y, al descender del acto venerable y del otro gemido, me reposo pensando en la marcha impertérrita del tiempo.

¿Por qué la cuerda, entonces, si el aire es tan sencillo? ¿Para qué la cadena, si existe el hierro por sí solo?

César Vallejo, el acento con que amas, el verbo con que escribes, el vientecillo con que oyes, sólo saben de ti por tu garganta.

César Vallejo, póstrate, por eso, con indistinto orgullo, con tálamo de ornamentales áspides y exagonales ecos.

Restitúyete al corpóreo panal, a la beldad; aroma los floreci-dos corchos, cierra ambas grutas al sañudo antropoide; repara, en fin, tu antipático venado; tente pena.

¡Que no hay cosa más densa que el odio en voz pasiva, ni más mísera ubre que el amor!

¡Que ya no puedo andar, sino en dos harpas!

¡Que ya no me conoces, sino porque te sigo instrumental, prolijamente!

¡Que ya no doy gusanos, sino breves!

¡Que ya te implico tánto, que medio que te afilas!

¡Que ya llevo unas tímidas legumbres y otras bravas!

In Short, I Have Nothing That Can Express My Life but My Death . . .

In short, I have nothing that can express my life but my death.

And, after all, at the end of a gradually ascending nature and of the sparrow as a whole, I sleep, hand in hand with my shadow.

And, as I descend from the venerable act and from the other lament, I rest mulling over the intrepid march of time.

Why the rope, then, if air is so simple? What is the chain for, if iron exists on its own?

César Vallejo, the accent with which you love, the word with which you write, the quiet wind with which you hear, know of you only through your throat.

César Vallejo, humble yourself, therefore, with ill-defined pride, with a nuptial bed of ornamental asps and hexagonal echoes.

Revive the corporeal honeycomb, beauty; aromatize flowering corks, close both grottos to the wrathful anthropoid; restore, in sum, your disagreeable deer; experience pain.

For there is nothing denser than hatred in the passive voice, nor a more grudging udder than love!

For now I cannot walk, except on two harps!

For now you know me only because, instrumental, I follow you so tediously!

For now I do not give worms but papal briefs!

For now I implicate you so deeply that you've thinned to half your size!

For now I am carrying a few vegetables, some timid and others brave!

Pues el afecto que quiébrase de noche en mis bronquios, lo trajeron de día ocultos deanes y, si amanezco pálido, es por mi obra: y, si anochezco rojo, por mi obrero. Ello explica, igualmente, estos cansancios míos y estos despojos, mis famosos tíos. Ello explica, en fin, esta lágrima que brindo por la dicha de los hombres.

¡César Vallejo, parece
mentira que así tarden tus parientes,
sabiendo que ando cautivo,
sabiendo que yaces libre!
¡Vistosa y perra suerte!
¡César Vallejo, te odio con ternura!

—*25 Noviembre 1937*

For the emotion that by night crushed my bronchia, occult deans brought by day, and, if I awake pale, it is for my work; and if I am red at nightfall, for my workman. All that explains, equally, this weariness of mine and these spoils, my famous uncles. All that explains, in sum, this tear I lift to toast the happiness of man.

César Vallejo, it seems
incredible that your relatives take so long,
knowing that I am captive,
knowing that you lie free!
Flamboyant, bitching luck!
César Vallejo, I hate you tenderly!

—November 25, 1937

Los desgraciados

Ya va a venir el día; da
cuerda a tu brazo, búscate debajo
del colchón, vuelve a pararte
en tu cabeza, para andar derecho.
Ya va a venir el día, ponte el saco.

Ya va a venir el día; ten
fuerte en la mano a tu intestino grande, reflexiona,
antes de meditar, pues es horrible
cuando le cae a uno la desgracia
y se le cae a uno a fondo el diente.

Necesitas comer, pero, me digo,
no tengas pena, que no es de pobres
la pena, el sollozar junto a su tumba;
remiéndate, recuerda,
confía en tu hilo blanco, fuma, pasa lista
a tu cadena y guárdala detrás de tu retrato.
Ya va a venir el día, ponte el alma.

Ya va a venir el día; pasan,
han abierto en el hotel un ojo,
azotándolo, dándole con un espejo tuyo . . .
¿Tiemblas? Es el estado remoto de la frente
y la nación reciente del estómago.
Roncan aún . . . ¡Qué universo se lleva este
    ronquido!

The Forsaken

Day is coming soon; wind
up your arm, look for yourself beneath
the mattress, stand again
on your head, so you can walk straight.
Day is coming soon, put on your jacket.

Day is coming soon; grasp
your large intestine firmly in your hand, reflect
before you meditate, for it is horrible
when misfortune falls on you
and a tooth falls out for good.

You need to eat, but, I tell myself,
don't feel sorrow, for sorrow and sobbing
beside a grave are not for the poor;
pull yourself together, remember,
trust in your white thread, smoke, call the roll
of your chain and store it behind your portrait.
Day is coming soon, put on your soul.

Day is coming soon; they're going by,
in the hotel they have opened an eye,
flogging it, beating it with a mirror of yours . . .
Are you trembling? It is the remote state of the brow
and the recent nation of the stomach.
They're still snoring . . . What a universe that snoring
  carries with it!

¡Cómo quedan tus poros, enjuiciandolo!
¡Con cuántos doses ¡ay! estás tan solo!
Ya va a venir el día, ponte el sueño.

Ya va a venir el día, repito
por el órgano oral de tu silencio
y urge tomar la izquierda con el hambre
y tomar la derecha con la sed; de todos modos,
abstente de ser pobre con los ricos,
atiza
tu frío, porque en él se integra mi calor, amada
    víctima.
Ya va a venir el día, ponte el cuerpo.

Ya va a venir el día;
la mañana, la mar, el meteoro, van
en pos de tu cansancio, con banderas,
y, por tu orgullo clásico, las hienas
cuentan sus pasos al compás del asno,
la panadera piensa en ti,
el carnicero piensa en ti, palpando
el hacha en que están presos
el acero y el hierro y el metal; jamás olvides
que durante la misa no hay amigos.
Ya va a venir el día, ponte el sol.

Ya viene el día; dobla
el aliento, triplica
tu bondad rencorosa
y da codos al miedo, nexo y énfasis,
pues tú, como se observa en tu entrepierna y siendo
el malo ¡ay! inmortal,
has soñado esta noche que vivías
de nada y morías de todo . . .

    —*Fin de Noviembre/Primera semana de Diciembre 1937*

Oh the state of your pores, bringing a judgment!
With so many twos, ay! you are so alone!
Day is coming soon, put on a dream.

    Day is coming soon, I repeat
through the oral organ of your silence
and urge taking the left with hunger
and taking the right with thirst; at any rate,
refrain from being poor with the rich,
warm
your cold, because my heat is blended with it, beloved
    victim.
Day is coming soon, put on your body.

    Day is coming soon;
morning, sea, meteor, are trailing
after your weariness, with banners,
and, because of your classic pride, hyenas
count their steps at the pace of the ass,
the bread lady is thinking of you,
the butcher is thinking of you, fingering
the cleaver in which are imprisoned
steel and iron and metal; never forget
that there are no friends during mass.
Day is coming soon, put on your sun.

    Day is coming now; double
your breath, triple
your rancorous goodness
and rub elbows with fear, nexus and emphasis,
for you, as observed in your crotch and as
evil, ay! is immortal,
have dreamed this night that you were living
from nothing and dying from everything . . .
                    —End of November/first week of December, 1937

¡Oh botella sin vino! ¡oh vino que enviudó de esta
    botella!
Tarde cuando la aurora de la tarde
flameó funestamente en cinco espíritus.
Viudez sin pan ni mugre, rematando en horrendos
    metaloides
y en células orales acabando.

¡Oh siempre, nunca dar con el jamás de tánto
    siempre!
¡oh mis buenos amigos, cruel falacia,
parcial, penetrativa en nuestro trunco,
volátil, jugarino desconsuelo!

¡Sublime, baja perfección del cerdo,
palpa mi general melancolía!
¡Zuela sonante en sueños,
zuela
zafia, inferior, vendida, lícita, ladrona,
baja y palpa lo que eran mis ideas!

Tu y él y ellos y todos,
sin embargo,
entraron a la vez en mi camisa,
en los hombros madera, entre los fémures, palillos;
tú particularmente,
habiéndome influido;

Oh Empty Bottle of Wine!
Oh Wine . . .

Oh empty bottle of wine! Oh wine made the widower
    of this bottle!
Late when the dawn of evening
flamed fatally in five spirits.
Widowerhood without bread or grime, terminating in
    horrendous metalloids
and ending in oral cells.

Oh always, do not ever engage with the never of so
    much always!
oh my good friends, cruel fallacy,
partial, piercing our truncate,
volatile, ohsomerry desolation.

Sublime, base perfection of the hog,
run your fingers over my accustomed melancholy!
Adz ringing in dreams,
adz,
asinine, inferior, sold out, lawful, thief,
bring down and feel what once were my ideas!

You and he and they and all,
however,
climbed into my shirt at the same time,
on my shoulders wood, between my femurs, toothpicks;
you particularly,
having influenced me;

él, fútil, colorado, con dinero
y ellos, zánganos de ala de otro peso.

¡Oh botella sin vino! ¡oh vino que enviudó de esta
botella!

—*16 Septiembre 1937*

he, futile, red, monied
and they, winged drones of a different weight.

Oh empty bottle of wine! Oh wine made the widower
of this bottle!

—September 16, 1937

Transido, salomónico, decente,
ululaba; compuesto, caviloso, cadavérico, perjuro,
iba, tornaba, respondía; osaba,
fatídico, escarlata, irresistible.

En sociedad, en vidrio, en polvo, en hulla,
marchóse; vaciló, en hablando en oro; fulguró,
volteó, en acatamiento;
en terciopelo, en llanto, replegóse.

¿Recordar? ¿Insistir? ¿Ir? ¿Perdonar?
Ceñudo, acabaría
recostado, áspero, atónito, mural;
meditaba estamparse, confundirse, fenecer.

Inatacablemente, impunemente,
negramente, husmeará, comprenderá;
vestiráse oralmente;
inciertamente irá, acobardaráse, olvidará.

—26 Septiembre 1937

Racked, Solomonic, Decent . . .

Racked, Solomonic, decent,
he wailed; composed, contemplative, cadaverous, perjured,
he left, he turned, he responded; he dared,
fatidic, scarlet, irresistible.

In society, in glass, in dust, in coal
he went away; he hesitated, speaking in gold; he glittered,
he turned around, in compliance;
in velvet, in tears, he fell back.

Remember? Insist? Go? Forgive?
Glowering, he would end up
flat on his back, gruff, astonished, mural;
he thought about imprinting himself, mingling, perishing.

Unassailably, unpunishably,
darkly, he will take the scent, he will understand;
he will dress himself orally;
uncertainly he will go, he will grow cowardly, he will forget.

—September 26, 1937

Alfonso: estás mirándome, lo veo,
desde el plano implacable donde moran
lineales los siempres, lineales los jamases
(Esa noche, dormiste, entre tu sueño
y mi sueño, en la rue de Riboutté)
Palpablemente,
tu inolvidable cholo te oye andar
en París, te siente en el teléfono callar
y toca en el alambre a tu último acto
tomar peso, brindar
por la profundidad, por mí, por ti.

Yo todavía
compro "du vin, du lait, comptant les sous"
bajo mi abrigo, para que no me vea mi alma,
bajo mi abrigo aquel, querido Alfonso,
y bajo el rayo simple de la sien compuesta;
yo todavía sufro, y tú, ya no, jamás, hermano!
(Me han dicho que en tus siglos de dolor,
amado sér,
amado estar,
hacías ceros de madera. ¿Es cierto?)

En la "boîte de nuit," donde tocabas tangos,
tocando tu indignada criatura su corazón,
escoltado de ti mismo, llorando
por ti mismo y por tu enorme parecido con tu
    sombra,

Alfonso: You Are Looking at Me, I'm Aware . . .

Alfonso: you are looking at me, I'm aware,
from the intractable plane on which dwell
linear evers, linear nevers.
(That night, you slept, between your dream
and mine, on rue Riboutté)
Palpably,
your unforgettable *cholo* hears you walking
in Paris, senses your voice fade from the telephone
and feels through the wire your last action
take on weight, toast
profundity, me, you.

    I still
purchase "du vin, du lait, comptant les sous"
beneath my overcoat, so my soul doesn't see me,
beneath that overcoat, dear friend Alfonso,
and beneath the simple beam from my compound temple;
I suffer still, and you, not now, never, my brother!
(I was told that in your centuries of pain,
cherished being,
cherished existing,
you made wooden zeroes. Is that true?)

    In the *boîte de nuit* where you played tangos,
your indignant child strumming its heart,
escorted by you yourself, weeping
for you yourself and for your great resemblance to your
    shadow,

monsieur Fourgat, el patrón, ha envejecido.
¿Decírselo? ¿Contárselo? No más,
Alfonso; eso, ya no!

El hôtel des Ecoles funciona siempre
y todavía compran mandarinas;
pero yo sufro, como te digo,
dulcemente, recordando
lo que hubimos sufrido ambos, a la muerte de ambos,
en la apertura de la doble tumba,
de esa otra tumba con tu sér,
y de ésta de caoba con tu estar;
sufro, bebiendo un vaso de ti, Silva,
un vaso para ponerse bien, como decíamos,
y después, ya veremos lo que pasa . . .

Es éste el otro brindis, entre tres,
taciturno, diverso
en vino, en mundo, en vidrio, al que brindábamos
más de una vez al cuerpo
y, menos de una vez, al pensamiento.
Hoy es más diferente todavía;
hoy sufro dulce, amargamente,
bebo tu sangre en cuanto a Cristo el duro,
como tu hueso en cuanto a Cristo el suave,
porque te quiero, dos a dos, Alfonso,
y casi lo podría decir, eternamente.

—9 Octubre 1937

Monsieur Fourgat, the *patron,* has aged.
Say that to him? Tell him? No.
Alfonso; that? Not now!

The Hotel des Écoles is always open
and they still buy mandarin oranges;
but I suffer, as I am telling you,
sweetly, remembering
what we have both suffered, at both of our deaths,
at the opening to the double tomb,
to that other tomb with your being,
and to this mahogany one with your existing;
I suffer, drinking a glass of your wine, Silva,
a glass to make us feel good, as we used to say,
and after, we'll see what happens . . .

And this is the other toast, among three,
melancholy, diverse
in wine, in world, in glass, the one we lifted
more than once to the body
and, less than once, to thought.
Today is even more different;
today I suffer sweetly, bitterly,
I drink your blood in reference to Christ the hard,
I chew your bone in reference to Christ the soft,
because I love you, two by two, yes, Alfonso,
and could almost say so, eternally.

—*October 9, 1937*

A lo mejor, soy otro; andando, al alba, otro que marcha
en torno a un disco largo, a un disco elástico:
mortal, figurativo, audaz diafragma.
A lo mejor, recuerdo al esperar, anoto mármoles
donde índice escarlata, y donde catre de bronce,
un zorro ausente, espúreo, enojadísimo.
A lo mejor, hombre al fin,
las espaldas ungidas de añil misericordia,
a lo mejor, me digo, más allá no hay nada.

Me da la mar el disco, refiriéndolo,
con cierto margen seco, a mi garganta;
¡nada, en verdad, más ácido, más dulce, más kanteano!
Pero sudor ajeno, pero suero
o tempestad de mansedumbre,
decayendo o subiendo, ¡eso, jamás!

Echado, fino, exhúmome,
tumefacta la mezcla en que entro a golpes,
sin piernas, sin adulto barro, ni armas,
una aguja prendida en el gran átomo . . .
¡No! ¡Nunca¡ ¡Nunca ayer! ¡Nunca después!

Y de ahí este tubérculo satánico,
esta muela moral de plesiosaurio
y estas sospechas póstumas,
este índice, esta cama, estos boletos.

—21 Octubre 1937

Possibly I Am Someone Else . . .

Possibly I am someone else; walking, at dawn, someone
    marching
around a large disk, a malleable disk;
fatal, figurative, audacious diaphragm.
Possibly, I think back as I wait, I take note of marbles
where scarlet sundial, and where bronze cot,
an absent, spurious, truly furious, fox.
Possibly, finally a man,
shoulders anointed with merciful indigo,
possibly, I tell myself, there is nothing beyond.

The disk gives me the sea, referring it,
with a certain dry margin, to my throat;
nothing, in truth, more acid, more sweet, more Kantian!
But another's sweat, but serum
or storm of meekness,
sinking or rising . . . that, never!

Reclining, refined, I exhume myself,
tumescent the mixture I beat my way into,
without legs, without mature clay, without arms,
a needle pinned in the great atom . . .
No! Never! Never yesterday! Never later!

And thence this satanic tubercle,
this plesiosaurian moral molar
and these posthumous suspicions,
this sundial, this gray hair, these tickets.

—October 21, 1937

Marcha nupcial

A la cabeza de mis propios actos,
corona en mano, batallón de dioses,
el signo negativo al cuello, atroces
el fósforo y la prisa, estupefactos
el alma y el valor, con dos impactos

al pie de la mirada; dando voces;
los límites, dinámicos, feroces;
tragándome los lloros inexactos,

me encenderé, se encenderá mi hormiga
se encenderán mi llave, la querella
en que perdí la causa de mi huella.

Luego, haciendo del átomo una espiga,
encenderé mis hoces al pie de ella
y la espiga será por fin espiga.

—*22 Octubre 1937*

Wedding March

In command of my own acts,
crown in hand, battalion of gods,
minus sign around my neck, unbearable
both match and haste, stultified
both soul and valor, with two impacts

right at the foot of the gaze; shouting;
limits, dynamic, fierce;
swallowing my imprecise weeping,

I will set fire to myself, as will my ant,
similarly my key, the quarrel
in which I lost the reason for my tracks.

Then, from the atom making a wheat head,
I will set fire to my scythes at its feet
and the wheat head will at last be a wheat head.

—*October 22, 1937*

La cólera que quiebra al hombre en niños,
que quiebra al niño en pájaros iguales,
y al pájaro, después, en huevecillos;
la cólera del pobre
tiene un aceite contra dos vinagres.

La cólera que al árbol quiebra en hojas,
a la hoja en botones desiguales
y al botón, en ranuras telescópicas;
la cólera del pobre
tiene dos ríos contra muchos mares.

La cólera que quiebra al bien en dudas,
a la duda, en tres arcos semejantes
y al arco, luego, en tumbas imprevistas;
la cólera del pobre
tiene un acero contra dos puñales.

La cólera que quiebra al alma en cuerpos,
al cuerpo en órganos desemejantes
y al órgano, en octavos pensamientos;
la cólera del pobre
tiene un fuego central contra dos cráteres.

                              —*26 Octubre 1937*

Anger That Breaks the Man into Boys . . .

The anger that breaks the man into boys,
that breaks the boy into birds of the same size,
and the bird, later, into little eggs;
the anger of the poor
has one oil against two vinegars.

The anger that breaks the trees into leaves,
the leaf into unequal buds
and the bud, into telescopic grooves;
the anger of the poor
has two rivers against many seas.

The anger that breaks good into doubts,
doubt, into three similar arcs
and the arc, then, into unexpected tombs;
the anger of the poor
has one sword against two daggers.

The anger that breaks the soul into bodies,
the body into dissimilar organs
and the organ, into eighth thoughts;
the anger of the poor
has one central fire against two craters.

                                        —*October 26, 1937*

¡Dulzura por dulzura corazona!
¡Dulzura a gajos, eras de vista,
esos abiertos días, cuando monté por árboles caídos!
Así por tu paloma palomita,
por tu oración pasiva,
andando entre tu sombra y el gran tezón corpóreo de tu
    sombra.

Debajo de ti y yo,
tú y yo, sinceramente,
tu candado ahogándose de llaves,
yo ascendiendo y sudando
y haciendo lo infinito entre tus muslos.
(El hotelero es una bestia,
sus dientes, admirables; yo controlo
el orden pálido de mi alma:
señor, allá distante . . . paso paso . . . adiós, señor . . .)

Mucho pienso en todo esto conmovido, perduroso
y pongo tu paloma a la altura de tu vuelo
y, cojeando de dicha, a veces,
repósome a la sombra de ese árbol arrastrado.

Costilla de mi cosa,
dulzura que tú tapas sonriendo con tu mano;
tu traje negro que se habrá acabado,
amada, amada en masa,
¡qué unido a tu rodilla enferma!

Sweetness Through Heart
Sweetness! . . .

Sweetness through heart sweetness!
Sweetness in clusters, you were vision,
those open days, when I rode through fallen trees!
Also through your dovely dove,
your passive prayer,
riding between your shadow and the bosomacious bulge of
    your shadow.

Beneath you and me,
you and me, sincerely,
your padlock choked with keys,
me climbing and sweating
and reaching infinity between your thighs.
(The hotel manager is a fool,
his teeth, admirable; I control
the pallid order of my soul;
Señor, way over there . . . I'm going, going . . . adiós, Señor . . .)

I think about all this, with emotion, everlastingly
and place your dove at the apogee of your flight,
and, limping along with happiness, sometimes,
I rest in the shadow of that dragged tree.

Rib of my thing,
sweetness that smiling you cover with your hand;
your black dress that must be ruined,
beloved, beloved en masse,
how attached to your ailing knee!

Simple ahora te veo, te comprendo avergonzado
en Letonia, Alemania, Rusia, Bélgica, tu ausente,
tu portátil ausente,
hombre convulso de la mujer temblando entre sus vínculos.

¡Amada en la figura de tu cola irreparable,
amada que yo amara con fósforos floridos,
quand on a la vie et la jeunesse,
c'est déjà tellement!

Cuando ya no haya espacio
entre tu grandeza y mi postrer proyecto,
amada,
volveré a tu media, haz de besarme,
bajando por tu media repetida,
tu portátil ausente, dile así . . .

—*1931/1937*

Simple I see you now, ashamed I understand you
in Lithuania, Germany, Russia, Belgium, your absent,
your movable absent,
convulsed man of the woman trembling within his bonds.

Beloved in the figure of your irreparable tail,
beloved whom I would love with flowery matches,
quand on a la vie et la jeunesse,
c'est déjà tellement!

When now there is no longer space
between your greatness and my last project,
beloved,
I will go back to your stocking, you mussed kiss me,
following down your repeated stocking,
your movable absent, put it that way . . .

—*1931/1937*

Ello es que el lugar donde me pongo
el pantalón, es una casa donde
me quito la camisa en alta voz
y donde tengo un suelo, un alma, un mapa de mi España.
Ahora mismo hablaba
de mí conmigo, y ponía
sobre un pequeño libro un pan tremendo
y he, luego, hecho el traslado, he trasladado,
queriendo canturrear un poco, el lado
derecho de la vida al lado izquierdo;
más tarde, me he lavado todo, el vientre,
briosa, dignamente;
he dado vuelta a ver lo que se ensucia,
he raspado lo que me lleva tan cerca
y he ordenado bien el mapa que
cabeceaba o lloraba, no lo sé.

Mi casa, por desgracia, es una casa,
un suelo por ventura, donde vive
con su inscripción mi cucharita amada,
mi querido esqueleto ya sin letras,
la navaja, un cigarro permanente.
De veras, cuando pienso
en lo que es la vida,
no puedo evitar de decírselo a Georgette,
a fin de comer algo agradable y salir,
por la tarde, comprar un buen periódico,
guardar un día para cuando no haya,

It's All Because the Place
Where I Put On . . .

It's all because the place where I put on
my trousers is a house where
I take off my shirt aloud
and where I have a floor, a soul, a map of my Spain.
Just now I was talking
about me to myself, and was setting
a very large loaf of bread on top of a small book
and I have, then, made the transfer, I have transferred,
wanting to hum a little, the right
side of life to the left side;
later, I have washed all over, my belly,
vigorously, with dignity;
I have turned around to see what is getting dirty,
I have scraped what carries me so close
and I have carefully put away the map that
was nodding or crying, I don't know which.

My house, unfortunately, is a house,
a floor, fortunately, where my beloved little spoon
with its inscription lives,
my dearest still unlettered skeleton,
a razor, an eternal cigarette.
Truly, when I ponder on
what life is,
I can't help telling Georgette about it,
with the idea of eating something agreeable and going out,
that evening, to buy a good newspaper,
to save a day for when there is none,

una noche también, para cuando haya
(así se dice en el Perú—me excuso);
del mismo modo, sufro con gran cuidado,
a fin de no gritar o de llorar, ya que los ojos
poseen, independientemente de uno, sus pobrezas,
quiero decir, su oficio, algo
que resbala del alma y cae al alma.

    Habiendo atravesado
quince años; después, quince, y, antes, quince,
uno se siente, en realidad, tontillo,
es natural, por lo demás ¡qué hacer?
¿Y qué dejar de hacer, que es lo peor?
Sino vivir, sino llegar
a ser lo que es uno entre millones
de panes, entre miles de vinos, entre cientos de bocas,
entre el sol y su rayo que es de luna
y entre la misa, el pan, el vino y mi alma.

    Hoy es domingo y, por eso,
me viene a la cabeza la idea, al pecho el llanto
y a la garganta, así como un gran bulto.
Hoy es domingo, y esto
tiene muchos siglos; de otra manera,
sería, quizá, lunes, y vendríame al corazón la idea,
al seso, el llanto
y a la garganta, una gana espantosa de ahogar
lo que ahora siento,
como un hombre que soy y que he sufrido.

                  —21 Noviembre 1937

a night too, for when there is one
(that's what they say in Peru—sorry);
similarly, I suffer with great caution,
so as not to yell or cry, since eyes,
independent of oneself, have their own want,
by that I mean, their function, something
that slips from the soul and falls into the soul.

Having passed through
fifteen years; after that, fifteen, and before that, fifteen,
one feels, in truth, a little silly,
it's natural, as for the rest, what to do!
And what to stop doing, which is worse?
Except to live, except to get
to be what one is among millions
of loaves, among thousands of wines, among hundreds of mouths,
among the sun and its beam that bounces off the moon
and among the mass, the bread, the wine, and my soul.

Today is Sunday and, because of that,
an idea comes to mind and weeping to my breast
and to my throat, like a great lump.
Today is Sunday, and all this
is centuries old; otherwise,
it might be Monday, and the idea would come to my heart,
and weeping to my brain,
and to my throat, a frightening desire to drown
what I am now feeling,
like a man that I am and that I have suffered.

—November 21, 1937

Sermón sobre la muerte

Y, en fin, pasando luego al dominio de la muerte,
que actúa en escuadrón, previo corchete,
párrafo y llave, mano grande y diéresis,
¿a qué el pupitre asirio? ¿a qué el cristiano púlpito,
el intenso jalón del mueble vándalo
o, todavía menos, este esdrújulo retiro?

¿Es para terminar,
mañana, en prototipo del alarde fálico,
en diabetis y en blanca vacinica,
en rostro geométrico, en difunto,
que se hacen menester sermón y almendras,
que sobran literalmente patatas
y este espectro fluvial en que arde el oro
y en que se quema el precio de la nieve?
¿Es para eso, que morimos tánto?
¿Para sólo morir,
tenemos que morir a cada instante?
¿Y el párrafo que escribo?
¿Y el corchete deísta que enarbolo?
¿Y el escuadrón en que falló mi casco?
¿Y la llave que va a todas las puertas?
¿Y la forense diéresis, la mano,
mi patata y mi carne y mi contradicción bajo la
    sábana?

¡Loco de mí, lovo de mí, cordero
de mí, sensato, caballísimo de mí!

Sermon on Death

And, finally, passing to the domain of death,
which acts as squadron, former shepherd's crook,
paragraph and key, large hand and dieresis,
what do they matter, the Assyrian desk, the Christian pulpit,
the intense pull of Vandal furniture
or, even less, this proparoxytonic withdrawal?

Is it in order to finish,
tomorrow, as a prototype of the phallic boast,
as diabetes and as white chamberpotty,
as a geometric face, as corpse,
that sermon and almonds become necessary,
that there are literally potatoes left over
along with this fluvial specter in which gold blazes
and in which the price of snow burns?
Is it for that, that we die so much?
Only to die,
do we have to die every instant?
And the paragraph I write?
And the deistic crook I lift high?
And the squadron in which my helmet failed?
And the key that opens all doors?
And the forensic dieresis, the hand,
my potato and my flesh and my contradiction beneath the
    sheet?

Maddened I am, wolve I am, lamb I am,
prudent and ultraequine I am!

¡Pupitre, sí, toda la vida; púlpito,
también, toda la muerte!
Sermón de la barbarie: estos papeles;
esdrújulo retiro: este pellejo.

De esta suerte, cogitabundo, aurífero, brazudo,
defenderé mi presa en dos momentos,
con la voz y también con la laringe,
y del olfato físico con que oro
y del instinto de inmovilidad con que ando,
me honraré mientras viva—hay que decirlo;
se enorgullecerán mis moscardones,
porque, al centro, estoy yo, y a la derecha,
también, y, a la izquierda, de igual modo.

—8 Diciembre 1937

Desk, yes, all my life long; pulpit,
that too, all my death long!
Sermon of barbarism: these papers;
proparoxytonic withdrawal: this skin.

   Like this, meditative, auriferous, strong-armed,
I will defend my prey at two moments,
with my voice and also with my larynx,
and using the sense of smell with which I pray
and the instinct of immobility with which I walk,
I shall do myself honor as long as I live—that must be said;
my horseflies will be filled with pride,
because, deep down, I am who I am, and to the right,
as well, and, to the left, in equal measure.

                                        —*December 8, 1937*

ESPAÑA, APARTA DE MÍ ESTE CÁLIZ /
SPAIN, TAKE THIS CHALICE FROM ME

I

Himno a los voluntarios de la República

Voluntario de España, miliciano
de huesos fidedignos, cuando marcha a morir tu corazón,
cuando marcha a matar con su agonía
mundial, no sé verdaderamente
qué hacer, dónde ponerme; corro, escribo, aplaudo,
lloro, atisbo, destrozo, apagan, digo
a mi pecho que acabe, al bien, que venga,
y quiero desgraciarme;
descúbrome la frente impersonal hasta tocar
el vaso de la sangre, me detengo,
detienen mi tamaño esas famosas caídas de arquitecto
con las que se honra el animal que me honra;
refluyen mis instintos a sus sogas,
humea ante mi tumba la alegría
y, otra vez, sin saber qué hacer, sin nada, déjame,
desde mi piedra en blanco, déjame,
solo,
cuadrumano, más acá, mucho más lejos,
al no caber entre mis manos tu largo rato extático,
quiebro contra tu rapidez de doble filo
mi pequeñez en traje de grandeza!

Un día diurno, claro, atento, fértil
¡oh bienio, el de los lóbregos semestres suplicantes,
por el que iba la pólvora mordiéndose los codos!
¡oh dura pena y más duros pedernales!
¡oh frenos los tascados por el pueblo!
Un día prendió el pueblo su fósforo cautivo, oró de cólera

I

Hymn to the Volunteers
of the Republic

Volunteer for Spain, militiaman
of trustworthy bones, when your heart marches to its death,
when it marches with its universal agony
to kill, I don't truly know
what to do, where to be; I run, write, applaud,
weep, observe, destroy, they extinguish, I tell
my breast to be numb, the good, to come,
and I want to bring disgrace upon myself;
I peel back my impersonal brow until I touch
the vessel of my blood, I stop,
my breadth impeded by those famed architect collapses
with which the animal that honors me is honored,
my instincts redound to their bonds,
joyful smoke rises before my tomb
and again without knowing what to do, having nothing, leave me,
from my unmarked stone, leave me,
alone,
quadrumanous, closer, farther beyond,
since my hands cannot contain your long rapture
I shatter against your two-edged fleetness
my pettiness dressed in a suit of greatness!

One everyday day, clear, alert, fecund,
O biennium, the one of the lugubrious supplicant months,
the one gunpowder moved through chewing its elbows!
O hard pain and harder flint beds!
O bits champed on by the people!
One day the people lit their captive match, choleric prayed

221

y soberanamente pleno, circular,
cerró su natalicio con manos electivas;
arrastraban candado ya los déspotas
y en el candado, sus bacterias muertas . . .

¿Batallas? ¡No! Pasiones. Y pasiones precedidas
de dolores con rejas de esperanzas,
de dolores de pueblos con esperanzas de hombres!
¡Muerte y pasión de paz, las populares!
¡Muerte y pasión guerreras entre olivos, entendámosnos!
Tal en tu aliento cambian de agujas atmosféricas los vientos
y de llave las tumbas en tu pecho,
tu frontal elevándose a primera potencia de martirio.

El mundo exclama: "¡Cosas de españoles!" Y es verdad.
    Consideremos,
durante una balanza, a quema ropa,
a Calderón, dormido sobre la cola de un anfibio muerto
o a Cervantes, diciendo: "Mi reino es de este mundo, pero
también del otro": ¡punta y filo en dos papeles!
Contemplemos a Goya, de hinojos y rezando ante un espejo,
a Coll, el paladín en cuyo asalto cartesiano
tuvo un sudor de nube el paso llano
o a Quevedo, ese abuelo instantáneo de los dinamiteros
o a Cajal, devorado por su pequeño infinito, o todavía
a Teresa, mujer, que muere porque no muere
o a Lina Odena, en pugna en más de un punto con Teresa . . .
(Todo acto o voz genial viene del pueblo
y va hacia él, de frente o transmitidos
por incesantes briznas, por el humo rosado
de amargas contraseñas sin fortuna)
Así tu criatura, miliciano, así tu exangüe criatura,
agitada por una piedra inmóvil,
se sacrifica, apártase,
decae para arriba y por su llama incombustible sube,
sube hasta los débiles,
distribuyendo españas a los toros,
toros a las palomas . . .

and sovereignly complete, circular,
closed their day of birth with elective hands;
despots already dragging padlock
and in the padlock, their dead bacteria . . .

Battles? No! Passions! And passions preceded
by sorrows with iron bars of hopes,
by sorrows of peoples with the hopes of man!
Death and passion of peace, the peoples'!
Death and passion of war amid the olive trees, let us agree on this!
As on your breath the winds shift atmospheric needles
and the key of the tombs in your breast,
your brow rising to the first power of martyrdom.

The world exclaims: "A Spanish affair!" And it's true.
  Let us consider,
during a weighing, point blank,
Calderón, asleep on the tail of a dead amphibian
or Cervantes, saying: "My kingdom is of this world,
but of the other as well"; tip and blade in two roles!
Let us reflect on Goya, on his knees and praying before a mirror,
Coll, the paladin in whose Cartesian assault
the paso llano raised a sweaty cloud
or Quevedo, that instantaneous grandfather of dynamiters
or Cajal, devoured by his small infinity, or still
Teresa, woman, who dies because she isn't dying
or Lina Odena, contesting more than one point with Teresa . . .
(Every act or affable voice comes from the people
or moves toward them, directly or transmitted
by uninterrupted filaments, by the rosy smoke
of bitter, luckless countersigns)
So too your child, militiaman, so too your bloodless child,
shaken by a motionless stone,
sacrifices itself, moves away,
decays upward and by way of its incombustible flame rises,
rises toward the weak,
distributing Spains to the bulls,
bulls to the doves . . .

Proletario que mueres de universo, ¡en qué frenética
   armonía
acabará tu grandeza, tu miseria, tu vorágine impelente,
tu violencia metódica, tu caos teórico y práctico, tu gana
dantesca, españolísima, de amar, aunque sea a traición, a
   tu enemigo!
¡Liberador ceñido de grilletes,
sin cuyo esfuerzo hasta hoy continuaría sin asas la
   extensión,
vagarían acéfalos los clavos,
antiguo, lento, colorado, el día,
nuestros amados cascos, insepultos!
¡Campesino caído con tu verde follaje por el hombre,
con la inflexión social de tu meñique,
con tu buey que se queda, con tu física,
también con tu palabra atada a un palo
y tu cielo arrendado
y con la arcilla inserta en tu cansancio
y la que estaba en tu uña, caminando!
¡Constructores
agrícolas, civiles y guerreros,
de la activa, hormigueante eternidad: estaba escrito
que vosotros haríais la luz, entornando
con la muerte vuestros ojos;
que, a la caída cruel de vuestras bocas,
vendrá en siete bandejas la abundancia, todo
en el mundo será de oro súbito
y el oro,
fabulosos mendigos de vuestra propia secreción de sangre,
y el oro mismo será entonces de oro!

¡Se amarán todos los hombres
y comerán tomados de las puntas de vuestros pañuelos tristes
y beberán en nombre
de vuestras gargantas infaustas!
Descansarán andando al pie de esta carrera,
sollozarán pensando en vuestras órbitas, venturosos

Proletarian who dies of the universe, in what frenzied
    harmony
will your grandeur end, your misery, your impelling vortex,
your methodical violence, your theoretical and practical
    chaos, your Dantesque, most Spanish, desire to love,
though it be by treachery, your enemy!
Liberator! bound with shackles,
without whose effort ungraspable expansion would
    continue,
nails would wander headless,
the day, ancient, slow, red,
our beloved helmets, unburied!
Peasant fallen for man with your green foliage,
with the social bent of your little finger,
with your remaining ox, with your configuration,
also with your word tied to a stick
and your rented sky
and with clay inserted in your weariness
and what was under your fingernail, walking!
Agricultural,
civilian and military builders
of the active, swarming eternity: it was written
that you would bring light, your eyes
half-closing in death;
that with the cruel fall of your mouths
would come abundance on seven trays, everything
in the world will be of sudden gold
and gold,
fabulous beggars of your own blood secretion,
and gold itself will then be gold!

All men will love one another
and will eat holding the tips of your sad kerchiefs
and will drink in the name
of your unfortunate throats!
They will rest walking along this road,
they will sob thinking of your orbits, they will

serán y al son
de vuestro atroz retorno, florecido, innato,
ajustarán mañana sus quehaceres, sus figuras soñadas y
    cantadas!

¡Unos mismos zapatos irán bien al que asciende
sin vías a su cuerpo
y al que baja hasta la forma de su alma!
¡Entrelazándose hablarán los mudos, los tullidos andarán!
¡Verán, ya de regreso, los ciegos
y palpitando escucharán los sordos!
¡Sabrán los ignorantes, ignorarán los sabios!
¡Serán dados los besos que no pudisteis dar!
¡Sólo la muerte morirá! ¡La hormiga
traerá pedacitos de pan al elefante encadenado
a su brutal delicadeza; volverán
los niños abortados a nacer perfectos, espaciales
y trabajarán todos los hombres,
engendrarán todos los hombres,
comprenderán todos los hombres!

¡Obrero, salvador, redentor nuestro,
perdónanos, hermano, nuestras deudas!
Como dice un tambor al redoblar, en sus adagios:
qué jamás tan efímero, tu espalda!
qué siempre tan cambiante, tu perfil!

¡Voluntario italiano, entre cuyos animales de batalla
un león abisinio va cojeando!
¡Voluntario soviético, marchando a la cabeza de tu pecho
    universal!
¡Voluntarios del sur, del norte, del oriente
y tu, el occidental, cerrando el canto fúnebre del alba!
¡Soldado conocido, cuyo nombre
desfila en el sonido de un abrazo!
¡Combatiente que la tierra criara, armándote
de polvo,
calzándote de imanes positivos,

prosper and at the sound
of your brutal, flowering, innate return
they will tomorrow reconcile their tasks, their dreamed
    and sung-of forms!

    The very same shoes will fit he who climbs
with no paths to his body
and he who descends to the shape of his soul!
Bound together the mute will speak, the maimed will walk!
The blind, by now returned, will see
and the deaf, throbbing, will hear!
The unschooled will know, the wise will know nothing!
The kisses you could not give will be given!
Only death will die! The ant
will bring bits of bread to the elephant chained
to its brutal sensibility; aborted children
will be born anew, perfect, spatial
and all men will work,
all men will beget,
all men will comprehend.

    Worker, savior, our redeemer,
forgive us, brother, our trespasses!
As a drum says in its drumroll, in its adagios:
what an ephemeral never, your back!
what a changing always, your side view!

    Italian volunteer, among whose battle animals
an Abyssinian lion limps along!
Soviet volunteer, marching in the lead of your universal breast!
Volunteers from the south, the north, the east
and you, the one from the west, closing the funereal song
    of the dawn!
Soldier we know, whose name
parades by in the sound of an embrace!
Combatant the earth might have raised, arming you
with dust,
shoeing you with positive magnets,

vigentes tus creencias personales,
distinto de carácter, íntima tu férula,
el cutis inmediato,
andándote tu idioma por los hombros
y el alma coronada de guijarros!
¡Voluntario fajado de tu zona fría,
templada o tórrida,
héroes a la redonda,
víctima en columna de vencedores:
en España, en Madrid, están llamando
a matar, voluntarios de la vida!

¡Porque en España matan, otros matan
al niño, a su juguete que se pára,
a la madre Rosenda esplendorosa,
a viejo Adán que hablaba en alta voz con su caballo
y al perro que dormía en la escalera.
Matan al libro, tiran a sus verbos auxiliares,
a su indefensa página primera!
Matan el caso exacto de la estatua,
al sabio, a su bastón, a su colega,
al barbero de al lado—me cortó posiblemente,
pero buen hombre y, luego, infortunado;
al mendigo que ayer cantaba enfrente,
a la enfermera que hoy pasó llorando,
al sacerdote a cuestas con la altura tenaz de sus
    rodillas . . .

¡Voluntarios,
por la vida, por los buenos, matad
a la muerte, matad a los malos!
¡Hacedlo por la libertad de todos,
del explotado y del explotador,
por la paz indolora—la sospecho
cuando duermo al pie de mi frente
y más cuando circulo dando voces—
y hacedlo, voy diciendo,
por el analfabeto a quien escribo,

your personal beliefs in force,
different in character, your rod, intimate,
immediate skin,
walking your language around on your shoulders
and your soul crowned with pebbles!
Volunteer whipped from your cold,
temperate, or torrid zone,
heroes in the round,
victim in a column of conquerors:
in Spain, in Madrid, the call is
for killing, volunteers of life!

Because in Spain they kill, others kill
the child, kill his run-down toy,
resplendent mother Rosenda,
old Adán who talked aloud with his horse
and the dog that slept on the steps.
They kill the book, they shoot at its auxiliary verbs,
at its defenseless first page!
They kill the exact circumstance of the statue,
the sage, his cane, his colleague,
the barber next door—possibly he cut me,
but a good man and, then, short of luck,
the beggar who yesterday was singing across the street,
the nurse who went by weeping today,
the priest with the tenacious height of his knees on his
    back . . .

Volunteers,
for life, for the good, kill
death, kill the bad!
Do it for the freedom of all,
for the exploited and the exploiter,
for a peace without pain—I suspect it
when I sleep at the foot of my brow
and more when I go around calling out—
and do it, I often say,
for the illiterate person to whom I'm writing,

por el genio descalzo y su cordero,
por los camaradas caídos,
sus cenizas abrazadas al cadáver de un camino!

Para que vosotros,
voluntarios de España y del mundo, vinierais,
soñé que era yo bueno, y era para ver
vuestra sangre, voluntarios . . .
De esto hace mucho pecho, muchas ansias,
muchos camellos en edad de orar.
Marcha hoy de vuestra parte el bien ardiendo,
os siguen con cariño los reptiles de pestaña inmanente
y, a dos pasos, a uno,
la dirección del agua que corre a ver su límite antes que
    arda.

for the barefoot genius and his lamb,
for the fallen comrades,
their ashes incorporated in the corpse of a road!

   So that all of you
volunteers for Spain and for the world, would come,
I dreamed that I was good, and it was to see
your blood, volunteers . . .
Of this comes great courage, great anxieties,
many camels of an age to pray.
Today blazing good is marching on your behalf,
following you with affection are reptiles with immanent
   eyelashes
and, at two steps, at one,
the course of water racing to see its limit before it burns.

II

Batallas

Hombre de Estremadura,
oigo bajo tu pie el humo del lobo,
el humo de la especie,
el humo del niño,
el humo solitario de dos trigos,
el humo de Ginebra, el humo de Roma, el humo de
      Berlín
y el de París y el humo de tu apéndice penoso
y el humo que, al fin, sale del futuro.
¡Oh vida! ¡oh tierra! ¡oh España!
¡Onzas de sangre,
metros de sangre, líquidos de sangre,
sangre a caballo, a pie, mural, sin diámetro,
sangre de cuatro en cuatro, sangre de agua
y sangre muerta de la sangre viva!

Estremeño, ¡oh, no ser aún ese hombre
por el que te mató la vida y te parió la muerte
y quedarse tan solo a verte así, desde este lobo,
cómo sigues arando en nuestros pechos!
Estremeño, conoces
el secreto en dos voces, popular y táctil,
del cereal: ¡que nada vale tánto
como una gran raíz en trance de otra!
¡Estremeño acodado, representando al alma en su retiro,
acodado a mirar
el caber de una vida en una muerte!

II

Battles

Man of Estremadura,
I hear the smoke of the wolf beneath your foot,
the smoke of the species,
the smoke of the child,
the solitary smoke of two heads of wheat,
the smoke of Geneva, the smoke of Rome, the smoke of
    Berlin
and that of Paris and the smoke of your painful appendix
and the smoke that, finally, comes from the future.
Oh life! Oh earth! Oh Spain!
Ounces of blood
meters of blood, liquids of blood,
blood on horseback, on foot, mural, without diameter,
blood of four by four, blood of water
and dead blood of the blood that lives!

Estremaduran, Oh, do not yet be that man
for whom life killed you and death gave birth to you
and stays only to see you this way, from this wolf,
how you keep plowing in our breasts!
Estremaduran, you know
the two-voiced secret, tactile and of the people,
of the grain: that nothing is as valuable
as one great root in another's crisis!
Rooted Estremaduran, representing the soul in its withdrawal,
rooted in order to watch
how a life fits in a death!

¡Estremeño, y no haber tierra que hubiere
el peso de tu arado, ni más mundo
que el color de tu yugo entre dos épocas; no haber
el orden de tus póstumos ganados!
¡Estremeño, dejásteme
verte desde este lobo, padecer,
pelear por todos y pelear
para que el individuo sea un hombre,
para que los señores sean hombres,
para que todo el mundo sea un hombre, y para
que hasta los animales sean hombres,
el caballo, un hombre
el reptil, un hombre,
el buitre, un hombre honesto,
la mosca, un hombre, y el olivo, un hombre
y hasta el ribazo, un hombre
y el mismo cielo, todo un hombrecito!

Luego, retrocediendo desde Talavera,
en grupos de a uno, armados de hambre, en masas de a uno,
armados de pecho hasta la frente,
sin aviones, sin guerra, sin rencor,
el perder a la espalda
y el ganar
más abajo del plomo, heridos mortalmente de honor,
locos de polvo, el brazo a pie,
amando por las malas,
ganando en español toda la tierra,
retroceder aún, ¡y no saber
dónde poner su España,
dónde ocultar su beso de orbe,
dónde plantar su olivo de bolsillo!

Mas desde aquí, más tarde,
desde el punto de vista de esta tierra,
desde el duelo al que fluye el bien satánico,
se ve la gran batalla de Guernica.

Estremaduran, and not to have land that knew
the weight of your plow, nor more world
than the color of your yoke between two eras; not to have
the order of your posthumous herds!
Estremaduran, you let me
see you from this wolf, to suffer,
to fight for all and to fight
so that the individual may be a man,
so that señores may be men,
so that everyone may be a man, and so that
even animals may be men,
the horse, a man,
the reptile, a man,
the vulture, an honest man,
the fly, a man, and the olive tree, a man
and even a slope, a man
and the sky itself, a fine little man!

Then, retreating from Talavera,
in groups of one, armed with hunger, in masses of one,
armed from chest to brow,
without airplanes, without war, without rancor,
carrying their having lost on their backs
and their having won
lower than the bullet, mortally wounded by honor,
crazed from dust, arm on foot,
forced to love,
winning all the earth in Spanish,
still falling back, and not knowing
where to put their Spain,
where to hide their orb-given kiss,
where to plant their pocket-size olive tree!

But from here, later,
from the vantage of this land,
from the mourning toward which satanic blood flows,
the great battle of Guernica is in sight.

¡Lid a priori, fuera de la cuenta,
lid en paz, lid de las almas débiles
contra los cuerpos débiles, lid en que el niño pega,
sin que le diga nadie que pegara,
bajo su atroz diptongo
y bajo su habilísimo pañal,
y en que la madre pega con su grito, con el dorso de una
    lágrima
y en que el enfermo pega con su mal, con su pastilla y su
    hijo
y en que el anciano pega
con sus canas, sus siglos y su palo
y en que pega el presbítero con dios!
¡Tácitos defensores de Guernica!
¡oh débiles! ¡oh suaves ofendidos,
que os eleváis, crecéis,
y llenáis de poderosos débiles el mundo!

En Madrid, en Bilbao, en Santander,
los cementerios fueron bombardeados,
y los muertos inmortales,
de vigilantes huesos y hombro eterno, de las tumbas,
los muertos inmortales, de sentir, de ver, de oír
tan bajo el mal, tan muertos a los viles agresores,
reanudaron entonces sus penas inconclusas,
acabaron de llorar, acabaron
de esperar, acabaron
de sufrir, acabaron de vivir,
acabaron, en fin, de ser mortales!

¡Y la pólvora fue, de pronto, nada,
cruzándose los signos y los sellos,
y a la explosión salióle al paso un paso,
y al vuelo a cuatro patas, otro paso
y al cielo apocalíptico, otro paso
y a los siete metales, la unidad,
sencilla, justa, colectiva, eterna!

A priori combat, unaccountable,
combat in peace, combat of weak souls
against weak bodies, combat in which the child strikes out,
without anyone's telling him to,
beneath his atrocious diphthong
and beneath his extremely useful diaper,
in which the mother strikes out with her scream, with the
    reverse side of a tear
and in which the sick man strikes out with his illness, with
    his pill and his son
and in which the old man strikes out
with his gray hair, his centuries, and his stick
and in which the priest strikes out with God!
Tacit defenders of Guernica!
O you weak! O gentle abused,
rise up, increase,
and fill the world with powerful weak!

In Madrid, in Bilbao, in Santander,
cemeteries were bombed,
and the immortal dead,
of vigilant bones and eternal shoulder, from the tombs,
the immortal dead, from feeling, seeing, hearing
how base the evil, how dead the vile aggressors,
then renewed their uncompleted grieving
they concluded weeping, concluded
hoping, concluded
suffering, concluded living,
concluded, finally, being mortals!

And the gunpowder was, suddenly, nothing,
intercrossing signs and seals,
and the explosion's passing drew out one step,
and the flight on four legs, another step
and the apocalyptic sky, another step
and the seven metals, unity,
simple, just, collective, eternal.

¡Málaga sin padre ni madre,
ni piedrecilla, ni horno, ni perro blanco!
¡Málaga sin defensa, donde nació mi muerte dando pasos
y murió de pasión mi nacimiento!
¡Málaga caminando tras de tus pies, en éxodo,
bajo el mal, bajo la cobardía, bajo la historia cóncava,
   indecible,
con la yema en tu mano: tierra orgánica!
y la clara en la punta del cabello: todo el caos!
¡Málaga huyendo
de padre a padre, familiar, de tu hijo a tu hijo,
a lo largo del mar que huye del mar,
a través del metal que huye del plomo,
al ras del suelo que huye de la tierra
y a las órdenes ¡ay!
de la profundidad que te quería!
¡Málaga a golpes, a fatídico coágulo, a bandidos, a
   infiernazos,
a cielazos,
andando sobre duro vino, en multitud,
sobre la espuma lila, de uno en uno,
sobre huracán estático y más lila,
y al compás de las cuatro órbitas que aman
y de las dos costillas que se matan!
¡Málaga de mi sangre diminuta
y mi coloración a gran distancia,
la vida sigue con tambor a tus honores alazanes,
con cohetes, a tus niños eternos
y con silencio a tu último tambor,
con nada, a tu alma,
y con más nada, a tu esternón genial!
¡Málaga, no te vayas con tu nombre!
¡Que si te vas,
te vas
toda, hacia ti, infinitamente toda en son total,
concorde con tu tamaño fijo en que me aloco,
con tu suela feraz y su agujero
y tu navaja antigua atada a tu hoz enferma

Málaga with no father or mother,
no little stone, no oven, no white dog!
Málaga with no defense, where my death was born taking
    steps
and my birth died of passion!
Málaga, walking behind your feet, in exodus,
below evil, below cowardice, below concave, unspeakable
    history,
with the yolk in your hand, organic land!
and the white on the tips of your hair: complete chaos!
Málaga fleeing
from father to father, familial, from your son to your son,
along the sea fleeing from the sea
across the metal fleeing from the bullet,
at the level of the soil fleeing from the earth
toward the orders, ay!
of the depths that loved you!
Málaga assailed by blows, fatidic clot, bandits, hellblasts,
heavenlashes,
walking over hard wine, in a multitude,
over lilac foam, one by one,
over static hurricane and more lilac,
and to the beat of the four orbits that love
and of the two ribs that kill each other!
Málaga of my diminutive blood
and my coloration from afar
life with a drum follows your reddish brown honors,
with rockets, your eternal children
and with silence your last drum,
with nothing, your soul,
and with more nothing, your genial sternum!
Málaga, do not leave with your name!
For if you go,
all of you
goes, toward you, infinitely all in total sound,
in concord with your defined size in which I am crazed
with your ferocious shoe sole and its hole
and your old knife strapped to your ailing scythe

y tu madero atado a un martillo!
¡Málaga literal y malagüeña,
huyendo a Egipto, puesto que estás clavada,
alargando en sufrimiento idéntico tu danza,
resolviéndose en ti el volumen de la esfera,
perdiendo tu botijo, tus cánticos, huyendo
con tu España exterior y tu orbe innato!
¡Málaga por derecho propio
y en el jardín biológico, más Málaga!
¡Málaga en virtud
del camino, en atención al lobo que te sigue
y en razón del lobezno que te espera!
¡Málaga, que estoy llorando!
¡Málaga, que lloro y lloro!

and your log bound to a hammer!
Literal and Malagüeñan Málaga,
fleeing toward Egypt, since you are transfixed,
drawing out in identical suffering your dance,
reducing within you the volume of the sphere,
losing your water pitcher, your songs, fleeing
with your external Spain and your innate orb!
Málaga for its own right
and in the biological garden, more Málaga!
Málaga in virtue
of the road, in awareness of the wolf that follows you
and because of the wolf cub that awaits you!
Málaga, I am weeping!
Málaga, I weep and I weep!

III

Solía escribir con su dedo grande en el aire:
"¡Viban los compañeros! Pedro Rojas,"
de Miranda de Ebro, padre y hombre,
marido y hombre, ferroviario y hombre,
padre y más hombre, Pedro y sus dos muertes.

Papel de viento, lo han matado; ¡pasa!
Pluma de carne, lo han matado: ¡pasa!
¡Abisa a todos compañeros pronto!

Palo en el que han colgado su madero,
lo han matado;
¡lo han matado al pie de su dedo grande!
¡Han matado, a la vez, a Pedro, a Rojas!

¡Viban los compañeros
a la cabecera de su aire escrito!
¡Viban con esta b del buitre en las entrañas
de Pedro
y de Rojas, del héroe y del mártir!

Registrándole, muerto, sorprendiéronle
en su cuerpo un gran cuerpo, para
el alma del mundo,
y en la chaqueta una cuchara muerta.

Pedro también solía comer
entre las criaturas de su carne, asear, pintar

III

He Used to Write in the Air with His Big Toe . . .

He used to write in the air with his big toe:
"Long liv the companyeros! Pedro Rojas,"
from Miranda de Ebro, father and man,
husband and man, railroad worker and man,
father and more man. Pedro and his two deaths.

Wind paper, they have killed him: *pasa!*
Flesh quill, they have killed him: *pasa!*
Adviz all companyeros quik!

Stick on which they have hung his log,
they have killed him;
they have killed him at the base of his big toe!
They have killed both at the same time, Pedro and
    Rojas!

"Long liv the companyeros
at the source of their inscribed air!"
Liv with this b of buzzard in Pedro's
gut
and Rojas's, and the hero and the martyr's too!
Searching him, dead, they surprised
a large body in his body, for
the soul of the world,
and in his jacket a dead spoon.

Pedro also used to eat
amid the children of his flesh, clean up, paint

la mesa y vivir dulcemente
en representación de todo el mundo.
Y esta cuchara anduvo en su chaqueta,
despierto o bien cuando dormía, siempre,
cuchara muerta viva, ella y sus símbolos.
¡Abisa a todos compañeros pronto!
¡Viban los compañeros al pie de esta cuchara para siempre!

Lo han matado, obligándole a morir
a Pedro, a Rojas, al obrero, al hombre, a aquél
que nació muy niñín, mirando al cielo,
y que luego creció, se puso rojo
y luchó con sus células, sus nos, sus todavías, sus hambres,
    sus pedazos.
Lo han matado suavemente
entre el cabello de su mujer, la Juana Vásquez,
a la hora del fuego, al año del balazo
y cuando andaba cerca ya de todo.

Pedro Rojas, así, después de muerto,
se levantó, besó su catafalco ensangrentado,
lloró por España
y volvió a escribir con el dedo en el aire:
¡Viban los compañeros! Pedro Rojas."
Su cadáver estaba lleno de mundo.

—7 Noviembre 1937

the table and live a sweet life
representing us all.
And this spoon traveled in his jacket,
awake or on toward when he slept, always,
dead live spoon, it and its symbols.
Adviz all companyeros quik!
Long liv the companyeros at the foot of this spoon forever!

They have killed him, forcing death on
Pedro, Rojas, the worker, the man, the one
who was born a mite of a thing, looking at the sky,
and who then grew, turned red
and fought with his cells, his noes, his stills, his hungers, his
    pieces.

They have killed him gently
in the hair of his wife, la Juana Vázquez,
at the hour of gunfire, the year of gunshot
and when he was already walking near everything.

Pedro Rojas, thus, after death,
rose, kissed his bloodstained catafalque,
wept for Spain
and again wrote with his toe in the air:
"Long liv the companyeros! Pedro Rojas!"

His corpse was filled with world.

—*November 7, 1937*

IV

Los mendigos pelean por España
mendigando en París, en Roma, en Praga
y refrendando así, con mano gótica, rogante,
los pies de los Apóstoles, en Londres, en New York, en
    Méjico.
Los pordioseros luchan suplicando infernalmente
a Dios por Santander,
la lid en que ya nadie es derrotado.
Al sufrimiento antiguo
danse, encarnízanse en llorar plomo social
al pie del individuo,
y atacan a gemidos, los mendigos,
matando con tan solo ser mendigos.

Ruegos de infantería,
en que el arma ruega del metal para arriba,
y ruega la ira, más acá de la pólvora iracunda.
Tácitos escuadrones que disparan,
con cadencia mortal, su mansedumbre,
desde un umbral, desde sí mismos, ¡ay! desde sí mismos.
Potenciales guerreros
sin calcetines al calzar el trueno,
satánicos, numéricos,
arrastrando sus títulos de fuerza,
migaja al cinto,
fusil doble calibre: sangre y sangre.
¡El poeta saluda al sufrimiento armado!

                              —*23 Octubre 1937*

IV

The Beggars Fight for Spain . . .

The beggars fight for Spain,
begging in Paris, in Rome, in Prague
and thus, with Gothic, imploring hand, authenticating
the feet of the Apostles, in London, in New York, in Mexico City.
The mendicants fight fiendishly entreating
God on behalf of Santander,
the conflict in which no one is yet defeated.
They give themselves
to age-old suffering, and goad themselves to cruelty by
    weeping societal lead
at the foot of the individual,
and moaning they attack, these beggars,
killing by the mere fact of being beggars.

Pleas of infantry,
in which the weapon pleads upwardness from the metal,
and anger pleads closer here to the wrathful gunpowder.
Tacit squadrons that fire,
with lethal cadence, their meekness
from a doorway, from themselves, ay! from themselves.
Potential warriors
sockless as they shoe the thunder,
satanic, numerous
dragging their diplomas of strength
a crumb at the belt,
dual caliber rifle: blood and blood.
The poet salutes armed suffering!

—*October 23, 1937*

V
Imagen española de la muerte

¡Ahí pasa! ¡Llamadla! ¡Es su costado!
¡Ahí pasa la muerte por Irún:
sus pasos de acordeón, su palabrota,
su metro del tejido que te dije,
su gramo de aquel peso que he callado . . . ¡si son ellos!

¡Llamadla! ¡Daos prisa! Va buscándome en los rifles,
como que sabe bien dónde la venzo,
cuál es mi maña grande, mis leyes especiosas, mis códigos
    terribles.
¡Llamadla! Ella camina exactamente como un hombre, entre
    las fieras,
se apoya de aquel brazo que se enlaza a nuestros pies
cuando dormimos en los parapetos
y se pára a las puertas elásticas del sueño.

¡Gritó! ¡Gritó! ¡Gritó su grito nato, sensorial!
Gritara de vergüenza, de ver cómo ha caído entre las plantas,
de ver cómo se aleja de las bestias,
de oír cómo decimos: ¡Es la muerte!
¡De herir nuestros más grandes intereses!

(Porque elabora su hígado la gota que te dije, camarada;
porque se come el alma del vecino)

¡Llamadla! hay que seguirla
hasta el pie de los tanques enemigos,
que la muerte es un ser sido a la fuerza,

V

Spanish Image of Death

There she goes! Call her! It's her side!
Death is passing through Irún:
her accordion steps, her cursing,
her meter of the cloth I told you about,
her gram of that weight I never told you about . . . if it's them!

Call her! Hurry! She's come looking for me among the
    rifles,
for she knows exactly where I defeat her,
what my best skill is, my specious laws, my terrible codes.
Call her! She is walking the way a man walks, among wild
    beasts,
she is braced on that arm that wraps around our feet
when we sleep on the parapets
and she stops at the elastic doors of sleep.
She screamed! She screamed! She screamed her innate,
    sensorial scream!
She'd scream from shame, from seeing how she has fallen
among the plants,
from seeing how far she is from the beasts,
from hearing how we say, It's death!
From harming our most precious interests!
(Because her liver is distilling the drop I told you of, comrade;
because she is devouring our neighbor's soul.)

Call her! We must follow her
right up to the enemy tanks,
for death is a to be forced to be a been,

cuyo principio y fin llevo grabados
a la cabeza de mis ilusiones,
por mucho que ella corra el peligro corriente
que tú sabes
y que haga como que hace que me ignora.

¡Llamadla! No es un ser, muerte violenta,
sino, apenas, lacónico suceso;
más bien su modo tira, cuando ataca,
tira a tumulto simple, sin órbitas ni cánticos de dicha;
más bien tira su tiempo audaz, a céntimo impreciso
y sus sordos quilates, a déspotas aplausos.
Llamadla, que en llamándola con saña, con figuras,
se la ayuda a arrastrar sus tres rodillas,
como, a veces,
a veces duelen, punzan fracciones enigmáticas, globales,
como, a veces, me palpo y no me siento.

¡Llamadla! ¡Daos prisa! Va buscándome,
con su coñac, su pómulo moral,
sus pasos de acordeón, su palabrota.
¡Llamadla! No hay que perderle el hilo en que la lloro.
De su olor para arriba, ¡ay de mi polvo, camarada!
De su pus para arriba, ¡ay de mi férula, teniente!
De su imán para abajo, ¡ay de mi tumba!

whose beginning and end I carry engraved
at the fore of my illusions,
however much she may run the current danger
as you know
and act as if she doesn't know me.

Call her! She is not a being, violent death,
but, barely, a brief event;
rather, her manner tends, when she attacks,
tends toward simple tumult, without orbits or chants of
    happiness;
rather, her audacious time tends toward an ambiguous
    centime
and her muted carats, toward despotic applause.
Call her, for in calling her with rage, with figures,
she is helped to drag her three knees,
as, at times,
at times, enigmatic, global fragments pain and perforate,
as, at times, I touch myself and feel nothing.

Call her! Hurry! She's come looking for me,
with her cognac, her ethical cheekbone,
her accordion steps, her cursing.

Call her! We must not lose the thread of my weeping for
    her.
Of her odor upward, ay, my dust, comrade!
Of her pus upward, ay, my ferule, lieutenant!
Of her magnet downward, ay, my tomb!

VI
Cortejo tras la toma de Bilbao

Herido y muerto, hermano,
criatura veraz, republicana, están andando en tu trono,
desde que tu espinazo cayó famosamente;
están andando, pálido, en tu edad flaca y anual,
laboriosamente absorta ante los vientos.

Guerrero en ambos dolores,
siéntate a oír, acuéstate al pie del palo súbito,
inmediato de tu trono;
voltea;
están las nuevas sábanas, extrañas;
están andando, hermano, están andando.

Han dicho: "Cómo! Dónde! . . . ," expresándose
en trozos de paloma,
y los niños suben sin llorar a tu polvo.
Ernesto Zúñiga, duerme con la mano puesta,
con el concepto puesto,
en descanso tu paz, en paz tu guerra.

Herido mortalmente de vida, camarada,
camarada jinete,
camarada caballo entre hombre y fiera,
tus huesecillos de alto y melancólico dibujo
forman pompa española, pompa
laureada de finísimos andrajos!

VI

Procession Following the Capture
of Bilbao

Wounded and dead, brother,
true child, republican, they are walking on your throne,
since your spine fell so famously;
they are walking, you in your pallid, lean, and annual age,
laboriously engrossed facing the winds.

Warrior in both sorrows,
sit down and listen, bed down at the foot of the sudden stick,
adjoining your throne;
turn around:
the new sheets are there, strange;
they are walking, brother, they are walking.

They have said: "How! Where! . . . ," expressing themselves
in fragments of dove
and the children climb without crying to your dust.
Ernesto Zúñiga, sleep with your hand set,
with your concept set,
resting, your peace, in peace your war.

Mortally wounded of life, comrade,
comrade horseman
comrade horse between man and beast,
your small bones of high and melancholy design
form Spanish pomp, laurel-crowned
pomp of finest rags!

Siéntate, pues, Ernesto,
oye que están andando, aquí, en tu trono,
desde que tu tobillo tiene canas.
¿Qué trono?
¡Tu zapato derecho! ¡Tu zapato!

—*13 Septiembre 1937*

So sit down, Ernesto,
hear how they've been walking, here, on your throne,
since the white hair grew on your ankle.
What throne?
Your right shoe! Your shoe!

—*September 13, 1937*

VII

Varios días el aire, compañeros,
muchos días el viento cambia de aire,
el terreno, de filo,
de nivel el fusil republicano.
Varios días España está española.

Varios días el mal
mobiliza sus órbitas, se abstiene,
paraliza sus ojos escuchándolos.
Varios días orando con sudor desnudo,
los milicianos cuélganse del hombre.
Varios días, el mundo, camaradas,
el mundo está español hasta la muerte.

Varios días ha muerto aquí el disparo
y ha muerto el cuerpo en su papel de espíritu
y el alma es ya nuestra alma, compañeros.
Varios días el cielo,
éste, el del día, el de la pata enorme.

Varios días, Gijón;
muchos días, Gijón;
mucho tiempo, Gijón;
mucha tierra, Gijón;
y mucho dios, Gijón,
muchísimas España ¡ay! Gijón.

VII

Several Days the Air,
Compañeros . . .

Several days the air, compañeros,
many days the wind shifts the air,
the terrain, blade sharp,
on the level of a republican rifle.
Several days Spain is Spanish.

Several days evil
mobilizes its orbits, abstains,
paralyzes its eyes listening to them.
Several days praying with naked sweat,
the militiamen hang themselves from the man.
Several days, the world, comrades,
The world is Spanish unto death.

Several days here the firing has died
and the body has died in its role as spirit
and the soul is already our soul, compañeros.
Several days the sky,
this sky, the day sky, the one like an enormous paw.

Several days, Gijón;
many days, Gijón;
a lot of time, Gijón;
a lot of land, Gijón;
and a lot of god, Gijón,
many, many Spains, ay! Gijón.

Camaradas,
varios días el viento cambia de aire.

—*5 Noviembre 1937*

Comrades,
several days the wind shifts the air.
—*November 5, 1937*

VIII

Aquí
Ramón Collar,
prosigue tu familia soga a soga,
se sucede,
en tanto que visitas, tú, allá, a las siete espadas, en Madrid,
en el frente de Madrid.

¡Ramón Collar, yuntero
y soldado hasta yerno de tu suegro,
marido, hijo limítrofe del viejo Hijo del Hombre!
Ramón de pena, tú, Collar valiente,
paladín de Madrid y por cojones; Ramonete,
aquí,
los tuyos piensan mucho en tu peinado!

¡Ansiosos, ágiles de llorar, cuando la lágrima!
¡Y cuando los tambores, andan; hablan
delante de tu buey, cuando la tierra!

¡Ramón! ¡Collar! ¡A ti! Si eres herido,
no seas malo en sucumbir; ¡refrénate!
Aquí,
tu cruel capacidad está en cajitas;
aquí,
tu pantalón oscuro, andando el tiempo,
sabe ya andar solísimo, acabarse;
aquí,

VIII
Here . . .

Here,
Ramón Collar,
your family continues, rope by rope,
one after the other,
while you are visiting, you, there, the seven swords, in Madrid,
on the Madrid front.

Ramón Collar, plowman
and soldier even son-in-law of your father-in-law,
husband, contiguous son of the old Son of Man!
Ramón of sorrow, you, valiant Collar,
paladin of Madrid by virtue of balls; Ramonete,
here,
we are thinking a lot about how you comb your hair!

Anxious, easily weeping, when the tear!
And when the drums, they walk; they talk
in front of your ox, when the earth!

Ramón! Collar! Here's to you! If you are wounded,
don't succumb badly; control yourself!
Here,
your capacity for cruelty is in little boxes;
here,
your dark trousers, time elapsing,
know already to walk entirely alone, to finish;
here,

Ramón, tu suegro, el viejo,
te pierde a cada encuentro con su hija!

¡Te diré que han comido aquí tu carne,
sin saberlo,
tu pecho, sin saberlo,
tu pie;
pero cavilan todos en tus pasos coronados de polvo!

¡Han rezado a Dios,
aquí;
se han sentado en tu cama, hablando a voces
entre tu soledad y tus cositas;
no sé quién ha tomado tu arado, no sé quién
fue a ti, ni quién volvió de tu caballo!

¡Aquí, Ramón Collar, en fin, tu amigo!
¡Salud, hombre de Dios, mata y escribe!

—*10 Septiembre 1937*

Ramón, your father-in-law, the old man,
loses you at each meeting with his daughter!

I will tell you that they have eaten your flesh here
not knowing,
your chest, not knowing,
your foot;
but they all think deeply on your footsteps crowned with
    dust!

They have prayed to God,
here;
they have sat on your bed, talking loudly
between your solitude and your belongings;
I don't know who has taken your plow, I don't know who
went to you, or who came back from your horse!

Here, Ramón Collar, finally, your friend!
Here's to you, man of God, kill and write.

                                            —*September 10, 1937*

IX
Pequeño responso a un héroe
de la República

Un libro quedó al borde de su cintura muerta,
un libro retoñaba de su cadáver muerto.
Se llevaron al héroe,
y corpórea y aciaga entró su boca en nuestro aliento;
sudamos todos, el hombligo a cuestas;
caminantes las lunas nos seguían;
también sudaba de tristeza el muerto.

Y un libro, en la batalla de Toledo,
un libro, atrás un libro, arriba un libro, retoñaba del cadáver.

Poesía del pómulo morado, entre el decirlo
y el callarlo,
poesía en la carta moral que acompañara
a su corazón.
Quedóse el libro y nada más, que no hay
insectos en la tumba,
y quedó al borde de su manga el aire remojándose
y haciéndose gaseoso, infinito.

Todos sudamos, el hombligo a cuestas,
también sudaba de tristeza el muerto
y un libro, yo lo vi sentidamente,
un libro, atrás un libro, arriba un libro
retoñó del cadáver ex abrupto.

—*10 Septiembre 1937*

IX

Brief Funeral Prayer for a Hero of the Republic

A book lay at the line of his dead waist,
a book sprouted from his dead corpse.
They carried the hero away
and corporeal and bitter his mouth entered on our breath;
we all sweat, humanavels on our backs;
walking moons followed behind us;
the dead man sweat from sadness.

And a book, in the battle of Toledo,
a book, behind a book, above a book, sprouted from the
   corpse.

Poetry of a royal purple cheekbone, between the saying it
and the not saying it,
poetry in the moral letter that might accompany
his heart.
The book stayed and nothing else, for there are no
insects in the tomb,
and not passing the edge of his sleeve, the air grew damp
becoming gaseous, infinite.

We all sweat, humanavels on our backs.
The dead man too sweat from sadness
and a book, I saw, feeling it deeply,
a book, behind a book, above a book
sprouted from the ex abrupto corpse.

—*September 10, 1937*

265

X

Invierno en la batalla de Teruel

¡Cae agua de revólveres lavados!
Precisamente,
es la gracia metálica del agua,
en la tarde nocturna en Aragón,
no obstante las construídas yerbas,
las legumbres ardientes, las plantas industriales.

Precisamente,
es la rama serena de la química,
la rama de explosivos en un pelo,
la rama de automóviles en frecuencia y adioses.

Así responde el hombre, así, a la muerte,
así mira de frente y escucha de costado,
así el agua, al contrario de la sangre, es de agua,
así el fuego, al revés de la ceniza, alisa sus rumiantes ateridos.

¿Quién va, bajo la nieve? ¡Están matando? No.
Precisamente,
va la vida coleando, con su segunda soga.

¡Y horrísima es la guerra, solivianta,
lo pone a uno largo, ojoso;
da tumba la guerra, da caer,
da dar un salto extraño de antropoide!
Tú lo hueles, compañero, perfectamente,
al pisar
por distracción tu brazo entre cadáveres;

X

Winter in the Battle of Teruel

Water's streaming from washed revolvers!
Precisely,
it is the metallic grace of water,
in the nocturnal afternoon in Aragon,
not withstanding the constructed herbs,
the burning vegetables, the industrial greeneries.

Precisely,
it is the serene branch of chemistry,
the branch of explosives in a hair,
the branch of automobiles in frequency and good-byes.

Thus the man replies, thus, to death,
thus he looks straight forward and listens from the side,
thus water, the opposite of blood, is from water,
thus fire, the reverse of ashes, curries its numb ruminants.

Who goes there, under the snow? Are they killing? No.
Precisely,
life goes swishing its tail, with its second rope.

And war is beyond horror, inciting,
it makes a person long, hollow-eyed;
war leads to tomb, leads to falling,
leads to taking a strange anthropoid jump!
You smell it, compañero, perfectly,
as you step on it,
for distraction your arm among corpses;

tú lo ves, pues, tocaste tus testículos, poniéndote rojísimo;
tú lo oyes en tu boca de soldado natural.

Vamos, pues, compañero;
nos espera tu sombra apercibida,
nos espera tu sombra acuartelada,
mediodía capitán, noche soldado raso . . .
Por eso, al referirme a esta agonía,
aléjome de mí gritando fuerte:
¡Abajo mi cadáver! . . . Y sollozo.

you see it, for you touched your testicles, blushing deeply;
you hear it in your natural soldier mouth.

   Let's go, then, compañero;
your cautioned shadow awaits us,
your billeted shadow awaits us,
noontime captain, nighttime common soldier.
That is why, when I refer to this agony,
I move away from myself yelling loud:
Down with my corpse! And I sob.

XI

Miré el cadáver, su raudo orden visible
y el desorden lentísimo de su alma;
le vi sobrevivir, hubo en su boca
la edad entrecortada de dos bocas.
Le gritaron su número: pedazos.
Le gritaron su amor: ¡más le valiera!
Le gritaron su bala: ¡también muerta!

Y su orden digestivo sosteníase
y el desorden de su alma, atrás, en balde.
Le dejaron y oyeron, y es entonces
que el cadáver
casi vivió en secreto, en un instante;
mas le auscultaron mentalmente, ¡y fechas!
lloráronle al oído, ¡y también fechas!

—*3 Septiembre 1937*

XI

I Looked at the Corpse . . .

I looked at the corpse, its swift visible order
and the unhurried disorder of its soul;
I saw it survive, there was in its mouth
the intermittent age of two mouths.
They shouted its number to it: pieces.
They shouted its love to it: that meant more!
They shouted its bullet to it: dead as well!

And its digestive order was maintained
and the disorder of its soul, some time ago, in vain.
They left it and listened to it, and it is then
that the corpse
nearly lived, secretly, an instant;
but mentally they auscultated it, and dates!
they wept into its ear, and again dates!

—September 3, 1937

XII
Masa

Al fin de la batalla,
y muerto el combatiente, vino hacia él un hombre
y le dijo: "No mueras, te amo tanto!"
Pero el cadáver ¡ay! siguió muriendo.

Se le acercaron dos y repitiéronle:
"No nos dejes! ¡Valor! ¡Vuelve a la vida!"
Pero el cadáver ¡ay! siguió muriendo.

Acudieron a él veinte, cien, mil, quinientos mil,
clamando: "Tánto amor, y no poder nada contra la muerte!"
Pero el cadáver ¡ay! siguió muriendo.

Le rodearon millones de individuos,
con un ruego común: "¡Quédate, hermano!"
Pero el cadáver ¡ay! siguió muriendo.

Entonces, todos los hombres de la tierra
le rodearon; les vio el cadáver triste, emocionado;
incorporóse lentamente,
abrazó al primer hombre; echóse a andar . . .

—*10 Noviembre 1937*

XII
Mass

At the end of the battle,
and the combatant dead, a man came toward him
and he said: "Don't die, I love you so much!"
But the corpse, ay! went on dying.

Two came toward him and they repeated:
"Don't leave us! Courage! Come back to life!"
But the corpse, ay! went on dying.

Twenty came to him, a hundred, a thousand, five hundred
thousand,
crying out: "So much love and powerless against death!"
But the corpse, ay! went on dying.

Millions of people gathered 'round him,
with a common plea: "Stay with us, brother!"
But the corpse, ay! went on dying.

Then every man on Earth
gathered 'round it: the corpse, sad, moved, saw them;
slowly it rose up,
it embraced the first man; it began to walk . . .

—*November 10, 1937*

273

XIII
Redoble fúnebre a los escombros de Durango

Padre polvo que subes de España,
Dios te salve, libere y corone,
padre polvo que asciendes del alma.

Padre polvo que subes del fuego,
Dios te salve, te calce y dé un trono,
padre polvo que estás en los cielos.

Padre polvo, biznieto del humo,
Dios te salve y ascienda a infinito,
padre polvo, biznieto del humo.

Padre polvo en que acaban los justos,
Dios te salve y devuelva a la tierra,
padre polvo en que acaban los justos.

Padre polvo que creces en palmas,
Dios te salve y revista de pecho,
padre polvo, terror de la nada.

Padre polvo, compuesto de hierro,
Dios te salve y te dé forma de hombre,
padre polvo que marchas ardiendo.

Padre polvo, sandalia del paria,
Dios te salve y jamás te desate,
padre polvo, sandalia del paria.

XIII

Funeral Drumroll for the Rubble of Durango

Father dust who rises from Spain,
God save, free, and crown you,
father dust who ascends from the soul.

Father dust who rises from fire,
God save you, shoe you, and give you a throne,
father dust who art in heaven.

Father dust, great-grandson of smoke,
God save you and ascend to infinity,
father dust, great-grandson of smoke.

Father dust in whom the just come to die,
God save you and return you to earth,
father dust in whom the just come to die.

Father dust who grows in palms,
God save you and clothe you in courage,
father dust, terror of nothingness.

Father dust, you who are composed of iron,
God save you and give you the form of man,
father dust who marches along in flames.

Father dust, sandal of the pariah,
God save you and never untie you,
father dust, sandal of the pariah.

Padre polvo que avientan los bárbaros,
Dios te salve y te ciña de dioses,
padre polvo que escoltan los átomos.

Padre polvo, sudario del pueblo;
Dios te salve del mal para siempre,
padre polvo español, padre nuestro.

Padre polvo que vas al futuro,
Dios te salve, te guíe y te dé alas,
padre polvo que vas al futuro.

—*22 Octubre 1937*

Father dust whom the barbarians drive away,
God save you and encircle you with gods,
father dust whom the atoms escort.

Father dust, shroud of the people,
God save you from evil forever,
Spanish father dust, our father.

Father dust who moves toward the future,
God save you, guide you and give you wings,
father dust who moves toward the future.

—*October 22, 1937*

XIV

¡Cúidate, España, de tu propia España!
¡Cúidate de la hoz sin el martillo,
cúidate del martillo sin la hoz!
¡Cúidate de la víctima apesar suyo,
del verdugo apesar suyo
y del indiferente apesar suyo!
¡Cúidate del que, antes de que cante el gallo,
negárate tres veces,
y del que te negó, después, tres veces!
¡Cúidate de las calaveras sin las tibias,
y de las tibias sin las calaveras!
¡Cúidate de los nuevos poderosos!
¡Cúidate del que come tus cadáveres,
del que devora muertos a tus vivos!
¡Cúidate del leal ciento por ciento!
¡Cúidate del cielo más acá del aire
y cúidate del aire más allá del cielo!
¡Cúidate de los que te aman!
¡Cúidate de tus héroes!
¡Cúidate de tus muertos!
¡Cúidate de la República!
¡Cúidate del futuro! . . .

—*10 Octubre 1937*

XIV

Be Wary, Spain, of Your Own Spain . . .

Be wary, Spain, of your own Spain!
Be wary of the sickle without the hammer,
Be wary of the hammer without the sickle!
Be wary of the victim who did not choose to be,
of the executioner who did not choose to be,
and of the indifferent who did not choose to be!
Be wary of he who, before the cock crows,
may deny you three times,
and of he who later did deny you three times!
Be wary of skulls without tibias,
and of tibias without skulls!
Be wary of the newly powerful!
Be wary of he who eats your corpses,
of he who devours, dead, your living!
Be wary of the one hundred percent loyal!
Be wary of the sky beyond the air
and be wary of the air beyond the sky!
Be wary of those who love you!
Be wary of your heroes!
Be wary of your dead!
Be wary of the Republic!
Be wary of the future!

—October 10, 1937

XV

España, aparta de mí este cáliz

Niños del mundo,
si cae España—digo, es un decir—
si cae
del cielo abajo su antebrazo que asen,
en cabestro, dos láminas terrestres;
niños, ¡qué edad la de las sienes cóncavas!
¡qué temprano en el sol lo que os decía!
¡qué pronto en vuestro pecho el ruido anciano!
¡qué viejo vuestro 2 en el cuaderno!

¡Niños del mundo, está
la madre España con su vientre a cuestas;
está nuestra maestra con sus férulas,
está madre y maestra,
cruz y madera, porque os dio la altura,
vértigo y división y suma, niños;
está con ella, padres procesales!

Si cae—digo, es un decir—si cae
España, de la tierra para abajo,
niños, ¡cómo vais a cesar de crecer!
¡cómo va a castigar el año al mes!
¡cómo van a quedarse en diez los dientes,
en palote el diptongo, la medalla en llanto!
¡Cómo va el corderillo a continuar
atado por la pata al gran tintero!
¡Cómo vais a bajar las gradas del alfabeto
hasta la letra en que nació la pena!

XV
Spain, Take This Chalice from Me

Children of the world,
if Spain falls—I mean, you hear that said—
if her arm,
her forearm, falls from the heavens, caught
in a halter lead between two terrestrial plates;
children, how old the age of sunken temples!
how early in the sun what I was telling you!
how soon in your breast the ancient noise!
how old your 2 in the notebook!

Children of the world, Mother Spain
is here with the burden of her womb;
our teacher is here with her ferules,
mother and teacher is here,
cross and wood, for she gave you height,
vertigo and division and sums, children;
she is with herself, judgment fathers!

If she falls—I mean, you hear that said—if Spain
falls down from the Earth,
children, how you will stop growing!
How the year will chastise the month!
How your teeth will stay at ten,
the diphthong in block letters, the medal in tears!
How the young lamb will still be
tied by the foot to the large inkwell!
How you will descend the steps of the alphabet
to the letter that gave birth to pain!

Niños,
hijos de los guerreros, entre tanto,
bajad la voz, que España está ahora mismo repartiendo
la energía entre el reino animal,
las florecillas, los cometas y los hombres.
¡Bajad la voz, que está
con su rigor, que es grande, sin saber
qué hacer, y está en su mano
la calavera hablando y habla y habla,
la calavera, aquélla de la trenza,
la calavera, aquélla de la vida!

    ¡Bajad la voz, os digo;
bajad la voz, el canto de las sílabas, el llanto
de la materia y el rumor menor de las pirámides, y aún
el de las sienes que andan con dos piedras!
¡Bajad el aliento, y si
el antebrazo baja,
si las férulas suenan, si es la noche,
si el cielo cabe en dos limbos terrestres,
si hay ruido en el sonido de las puertas,
si tardo,
si no veis a nadie, si os asustan
los lápices sin punta, si la madre
España cae—digo, es un decir—
salid, niños del mundo; id a buscarla! . . .

Children,
sons of warriors, in the meantime,
speak softly, for at this very moment Spain is distributing
energy among the animal kingdom,
the flowers, the comets, and man.
Speak softly, for she is here
in all her rigor, which is great, not knowing
what to do, and in her hand
is the skull, speaking, it speaks and speaks,
the skull, the one with the braid,
the skull, the one from life!

Speak softly, I say to you:
speak softly, the song of syllables, the sobbing
of matter and the lesser murmur of the pyramids, and even
that of your temples walking with two stones!
Breathe softly, and if
a forearm falls,
if ferules clatter, if it is night,
if the sky can be held within two terrestrial limbs,
if there is noise in the sound of doors
if I am late,
if you see no one, if you are frightened
by pencils with dull points, if Mother
Spain falls—I mean, you hear that said—
go forth, children of the world; go out to seek her!

Index of Titles and First Lines